MENTORING HEROES

MENTORING HEROES

52 Fabulous Women's Paths to Success and the Mentors Who Empowered Them

Mary K. Doyle

3E Press

MENTORING HEROES
52 Fabulous Women's Paths to Success and the Mentors Who Empowered Them

Published by:
> **3E Press**
> PO Box 1004
> Batavia, IL 60510-1004

> Three E Press@aol.com

Printed in the United States of America

Publisher's Cataloging-in-Publication
(Provided by Quality Books, Inc.)

Doyle, Mary K.
    Mentoring heroes : 52 fabulous women's paths to success and the mentors who empowered them / Mary K. Doyle. -- 1st ed.
    p. cm.
    Includes index.
    LCCN: 99-97451
    ISBN: 0-9677449-2-X

    1. Mentoring. 2. Success. 3. Women in the professions. 4. Leadership.   I. Title.

BF637.S4D69 2000   158'.3
                    QB199-500570

*This book is dedicated to the mentor in all of us.
Bless this part that reaches out to others
to share wisdom and encouragement.*

In Loving Memory of My Mother:

Patricia M. Doyle

1928 – 1999

Disclaimer

MENTORING HEROES: 52 Fabulous Women's Paths to Success and the Mentors Who Empowered Them is a compilation of personal experiences. The many names of people and organizations mentioned are stated as a way to honor the gift of mentoring they generously shared.

The purpose of this book is to empower, enlighten, and entertain. The author and 3E Press shall have neither liability nor responsibility to any person or entity with respect to any loss or damage caused, or alleged to be caused, directly or indirectly by the information contained in this book.

If you do not wish to be bound by the above, you may return this book to the publisher for a full refund.

Table of Contents

ACKNOWLEDGMENTS

The Fabulous Fifty-Two women who took time from their very busy schedules to share their stories and their wisdom with me have my sincerest gratitude. Since I started my research for this book, these women have been a part of me. Not a day goes by that I don't think of them, their experiences, and what I have learned from them. They always will be in my prayers.

Thank you to Dr. Monique Anawis, Marcia E. Balestri, Kathy Ballman, Allison Barnett, Dr. Helen L. Bonny, Patricia Doyle Brewer, Victoria Bush-Joseph, Judy Chaffee, Anna Cheng Catalano, Ruth A. Chodak, Susan Coe Heitsch, Dr. Amy Coene Bales, Dr. Cheryl Conover, Margaret Cotterill, Janet Faye Damm, Susan Darby, Louise Dimiceli-Mitran, Diana Dionisio-Pieczynski, Emily K. Emmerman, Ruby M. H. Frank, Kathleen S. Freeland, Harriet Gerber Lewis, Linaya Hahn, Carol Havey, Jane Hayden, Dr. Susan M. Holstein, Ann Jillian, Barbara J. Junceau, Eta-Lyn Lampert, Dr. Ruth Martens, Dr. Jeannette B. Martens Sorrentino, Debra McElroy, Dr. Theresa McNally, Carole Miller, Sandy Oler, Teresa Orman, Dr. Diana Craig Patch, Sister Mary Stella Schellenberger, Susan Schreter, Laurie Scordo, Ingrid Sharos, Linda Shepard, Anita Smith, Rev. M. Sue Storm, Pamela J. Sullivan, Marlene Tighe, Debra Trent, Alice Umbach, The Honorable Hollis L. Webster, Leslie Wheeler Hortum, Dr. Nancy Wilson Dickey, and Rabbi Deborah Zecher.

11

ACKNOWLEDGMENTS

Thank you to the people who connected me to one of the Fabulous Fifty-Two. Thank you to Dr. Jeannette Martens Sorrentino for referring Dr. Amy Coene Bales. Thank you to Louise Dimiceli-Mitran for connecting me with Dr. Helen Bonny and Dr. Theresa McNally. Thank you to Mark Holstein for connecting me with Anna Cheng Catalano. Thank you to Barbara Junceau for connecting me with Judy Chaffee and Laurie Scordo. Thank you to Emily Emmerman for connecting me with Ruth Chodak. Thank you to Mary Lou Newstead for referring Dr. Cheryl Conover. Thank you to Patricia Doyle Brewer for connecting me with Susan Darby.

Thank you to Helen Hoge for referring Ruby Frank and Kathleen Freeland. Thank you to Diana Dionisio-Pieczynski for connecting me with Jane Hayden. Thank you to Teresa Orman for referring Sandy Oler. Thank you to Debra McElroy for referring Ingrid Sharos. Thank you to Marshall Brodien for referring Anita Smith. Thank you to Marcia Balestri for referring Pamela Sullivan. Thank you to Judy Chaffee for referring Marlene Tighe. Thank you to Sue Shivers for referring Vicky Bush-Joseph. Thank you to Rev. M. Sue Storm for connecting me with Alice Umbach. Thank you to James and Tina Baum for leading me to Rabbi Deborah Zecher.

A heartfelt thank you to the great networker, Dr. Herb Sohn, for not only connecting me with Dr. Monique Anawis, Dr. Nancy Wilson Dickey, Emily Emmerman, Harriet Gerber Lewis, Susan Schreter, and Leslie Wheeler Hortum but also for believing in me and this project. His supportive phone calls validated my personal desire to pursue this publication.

I am very grateful to those who helped me with publication and promotion. Thank you to Gigi Smith and Hunter Tylo for sharing their powerful media contacts. Thank you

ACKNOWLEDGMENTS

Aye Jaye for schmoozing publishers and agents on my behalf. I also thank Aye Jaye, Allison Barnett, Chuck Romano, and Joe Vitale for mentoring me in the business of publishing.

Several women proofread and commented on my work-in-progress. Thank you to my daughter, Erin Cannella, my sister, Patti (Patricia) Doyle Brewer, and my friends, Dr. Susan Holstein and Barbara Junceau for taking so much of their precious time to read page after page of this book. Thank you to Allison Barnett for designing the beautiful dust cover that reflects the essence of this book.

I have been richly blessed with a powerful network of mentors throughout my life. Thank you to all my relatives, friends, neighbors, coworkers, bosses, and teachers who reached out to me and participated in my personal and professional growth. And for daily doses of love and support I thank my husband Marshall; children Lisa, Erin, and Joseph; stepchildren and children-in-law Anita, Michael, Marshall, Caroline, Christine, and Paul; step-grandchildren Anna, Michael, Matthew, and Angela; father John Doyle; brothers Mike (John Michael) Doyle and Jimmy Doyle; sisters Patti Brewer and Margaret Cotterill; brother-in-laws Parke Brewer and Jimmy Cotterill; and dear friend Patty Cannella.

On behalf of The Fabulous-Fifty Two, I thank all the mentors who touched their lives. So many of you could not be mentioned in this book, but all are remembered and treasured for sharing their gifts.

Also thank you, the reader, for caring enough about mentoring, networking, sharing, and personal development to read *MENTORING HEROES*.

Native American people say we are all connected, we are all one. Mentoring is an example of this melting and meshing of peoples. Every one of The Fabulous Fifty-Two,

ACKNOWLEDGMENTS

my mentors, family, and friends have invested a part of themselves into me, and subsequently, into this book. As you read the following pages the words, thoughts, and personalities you consume will become a part of you. Hopefully, you will continue to pass on anything you may learn from us to your protégés, connecting you, and us together.

MENTORING IS:

- an opportunity to empower.

- being a sounding board.

- supporting a protégé's growth
  at their own pace
  and in their own way.

- sharing your stories.

- teaching an eager student
  what you have learned.

- creating opportunities
  for someone to succeed.

- introducing your protégé
  to other helpful people.

- allowing your protégé
  to accept the accolades
  for work they did
  with your assistance.

- trusting someone
  with your wisdom.

- non-judgemental.

MENTORING IS

- recognizing a protégé's
  talents and gifts
  before they do.

- watching someone
  exceed your level
  because of you.

- challenging your protégé
  to take that next leap.

- encouraging a protégé to fly.

- catching someone
  before they fall.

- rewarding.

- revealing a better,
  brighter, path.

- sharing your gifts,
  your time,
  your knowledge,
  and your wonderful, talented self.

PREFACE

We get to the top so much faster and easier with a little help from our friends. As a professional writer of newspaper feature articles, publicity, and advertising, I have had the privilege of interviewing several hundred people. Many of these people have overcome great personal or professional challenges to become strong, successful, and productive. Their journeys to success are diverse, but one point they often stress is that they did not walk that journey alone. Most successful people eagerly acknowledge that there were individuals in their lives who acted as catalysts for change and growth. They relied on these mentors for guidance, role modeling, and networking.

The significance of mentoring was reinforced during my studies for a Bachelor of Arts degree in Business Management and Leadership that I received in 1997. Examples of mentoring and its value in business was covered repeatedly in the required course work, but I felt the textbook and handbook information on how mentoring should be done was rigid. The guidelines certainly wouldn't work in my life-style. Nor did I think it would work in most other women's lives, either.

Women venture out into the world under different circumstances and with different priorities than men do. We work around soccer games, parent-teacher meetings, family dental visits, laundry, grocery shopping, and taking elderly parents to the doctor. Staying after work hours for a mentoring session typically doesn't fit into our schedules.

PREFACE

I started asking other women if they had been mentored, how they were mentored, and if they mentor. Their responses are fascinating and the essence of *MENTORING HEROES: 52 Fabulous Women's Paths to Success and the Mentors Who Empowered Them.* These women are leaders and role models who have been mentored by leaders and who mentor future leaders. They span a wide range of professions including scientists, artists, entrepreneurs, managers, educators, as well as spiritual, physical, and emotional healers. Their ages are from the late twenties to late seventies. All have completed either trade school or some undergraduate course work. Most have a bachelor's degree. Many have masters, doctorates, or medical degrees.

Some of these women I know very well, like my sisters Patti (Patricia) Doyle Brewer and Margaret Cotterill. Others I have worked with or seen on occasion. More than half of the women in this book I have yet to meet face-to-face, however I do feel a connection to all of them. They have been my partners on this journey, and I am ever so honored that they shared so much of themselves with me and for you.

Please keep in mind, this book offers only a representation of our country's most interesting and successful women. So many more reside and work with us every day. And not all of the mentoring experiences of these 52 women are included in this book. If you believe you played a significant role in any of these women's lives and were not mentioned, please do not feel offended. I was probably told about you. I apologize for not being able to include your story.

Also, my concentration on women's experiences in no way suggests that the benefits of mentoring only pertains to women. Neither does this concentration suggest that men can not, or have not, played critical roles in mentoring

18

women. You will find a majority of men named as mentors, men who have assisted these successful women greatly in their development.

I pass on these stories of personal mentoring experiences to you so that you may pick and choose from this collection and develop your own mentoring experiences. You are like no one else. Therefore, you do not want to identically copy any of these experiences or a step-by-step approach to mentoring. Rather, I suggest you might learn from the following stories and modify them to fit your needs and life-style.

In addition to working with a mentor, after reading *MENTORING HEROES* I hope you will be inspired to extend yourself to mentor the people around you. I challenge you to be a leader who promotes and builds other leaders, because in doing so, together we can make the world a better place.

My friend, Dr. Herb Sohn, quotes his father, Maurice Sohn, saying, "one person alone can not solve the problems of the world. But that one person can reach out to the next, who reaches out to the next, and together solve those problems."

You don't live in a world all alone. Your brothers are here too.

Albert Schweitzer on receiving the Nobel Prize
(1952)

Chapter One

LEADERSHIP
UP CLOSE AND PERSONAL

A pond ripples long after the stone has been tossed. The chime of a bell lingers after it has been rung. A star shines radiantly after it ceases to exist. Memories of pain and joy remain throughout our lives.

We are not alone in this world. Everything we think, say, and do radiates and ripples out to not only everyone around us, but also everyone around those people. When we succeed, the success belongs to all of us. When we fail, everyone around us fails.

We celebrate our alma mater's win in a band competition, our city's basketball championship, and our nation's Olympic gold medals. Also, we are ashamed as a family when our brother cannot hold a job, as a community when our neighbor abuses his partner, and as a nation when we destroy one another as in the Oklahoma bombing.

Leaders have the power to change the course of history. They are the recipient of their followers' trust, protection, labors, and/or money. Leaders envision a future few others see, develop a path to that future destination, and motivate others to follow their lead. They create ripples by challenging beliefs and encouraging personal and professional growth.

As parents, siblings, neighbors, co-workers, and friends we all are leaders to some degree. We have the capacity to create a ripple by changing the direction of a corporation, congregation, community, or family. Bringing fresh baked goods to a new neighbor more than welcomes that neighbor. By doing so, we clear a pathway to the community. Petitioning our neighbors and speaking to parent/teacher groups about school bus safety leads a community to safer transportation for our children. Covering for a co-worker home with a sick child sets a corporate precedent to work as one team and not as an individual. These steps may appear to be small, but they lead a community toward a positive path in progress.

I come from a very large, close family. When my mother was seriously ill in 1996, her care was not left solely to me, my siblings, and father. All of my relatives came forward to care for her. The weight of her care rippled across my father, myself, two sisters, two brothers, two brother-in-laws, my children, aunts, uncles, cousins, and all of their families, just as my mother's love had always done. What could have been an unbearable time, became an opportunity to reinforce our bonds as a family. My mother was the matriarch of our family, but each one of us took on a leadership role in varying degrees and arenas. We elevated each other individually and as a unit to a higher level.

Just as that small stone thrown in the pond ripples across the water, no action is so small that goes unnoticed or ineffective. If we all are responsible leaders who assist prospective leaders in their development, we also would be the recipient of the goodness reflected from these newly developed leaders. What we do for them comes back to us tenfold.

Imagine a world that continuously ripples with successes, accomplishments, generosity, and goodness. I believe that vision is a viable reality. I believe we can make that vision happen.

Leadership Potential

We know leaders when we see them, because we either watch others follow or are drawn to follow their instruction or example. We recognize the roles they play in leading humanity down a path different from the one people of their time were going. Galileo led our eyes to the heavens. Abraham Lincoln led a nation out of slavery. Henry Ford offered us the means to physically reach one another easier and faster than ever before. Mother Theresa directed our attention to the needs of the sick and poor. And Elvis Presley literally had us dancing to the beat of a different drummer. Perhaps, eventually we would have followed someone else in any of those directions, but we didn't. Those were the leaders we followed.

Researchers have identified a number of characteristics prevalent in leaders. Most leaders have a strong sense of vision and intuition. Communication and listening skills are superior. They also have a high energy level, the ability to function under stress, and the courage to think independently.

Leaders must be able to handle living with the double-edged sword of the role. They are admired and loathed, respected and scrutinized, loved and hated. They are emulated and envied. They are for the people, but never of the people, which promotes periods of isolation and loneliness.

It's essential for leaders to have charisma. The perfect political candidate will never win without a hefty dose of charm. Followers must be attracted to them to believe in their goals and be persuaded to follow. Bill Clinton's charisma attracted the voters to support him for a second term even though he had a questionable personal life. On the other hand, Ross Perot may have had the answers to pull this country out of financial debt but lacked the charisma it took to draw the votes.

Leaders must have the ability and courage to think and act in their own way. Diana Craig Patch, Ph.D., Archeologist Specializing in Ancient Egyptian Culture and Gallery Administrator at the Metropolitan Museum of Art in New York City, has been interested in archeology since age seven. Her characteristics of an independent thinker and the courage to pursue goals unlike the mainstream existed in her from the beginning. In junior high school, Diana was an achiever who did what she did and thought what she wanted while the rest of the girls her age were concerned with makeup, boys, and parties. She had the strength and self-confidence to think for herself from an early age, which may be why she was able to pursue and succeed on a path few people choose.

All the elements may be there, but what the individual does with leadership potential is a matter of choice. Some leaders are more memorable for leading their people to destruction rather than glory. History has shown us the dark side of leadership through the motivation of rulers such as Adolph Hitler and Saddam Hussein. Perhaps the prevalence of youth gangs, not only in our nation, but also across the globe, is related to that dark side of leadership and the need to belong.

According to a survey conducted in 1995 by the Office of Juvenile Justice and Delinquency Prevention's National

Youth Gang Center, 23,388 gangs and 664,906 gang members were estimated to reside in the jurisdiction of 2,007 law enforcement agencies in the United States. And these numbers are thought to be increasing. This situation is an outcry for opportunities for our children to belong to groups in which they can lead and be lead in a positive manner.

Most leaders aspire to the position long before they have the opportunity to lead. The sense of destiny and desire to attain power and achievement lies dormant waiting for the right time and place to come forward. Pamela J. Sullivan, Senior Vice President of TRW, Inc. said leadership potential can be identified as early as preschool. "As a child, I used to get so bossy no one would want to play with me," she said. "I reminded the others of the rules and always had to win."

Pamela excelled academically and socially. She held positions of authority such as president of the student body. With age, experience, and maturity, Pamela said her leadership style evolved considerably. She is no longer a domineering figure but rather an assistant in the development of potential leaders. "I enjoy sharing power and data, which is power in business. I feel good about myself as others grow," Pamela said.

Businesses, universities, and agencies across the country are concerned with the development of leadership. Courses, seminars, and workshops are being offered to encourage managers to participate in assisting with the growth of future leaders. Government agencies and hospitals are hosting mentoring programs. Area businesses are asked to allow employees time off to mentor elementary school students during school time.

The United States Air Force also realizes the significance in molding leadership characteristics. In a March 1996 issue of *Air Force Times*, Sheila Widnall states in an article, "Building Leadership - Step by Step," that the Air Force carefully observes candidates for leadership potential, then offers training to promote these upcoming leaders. These steps are concerned with a fair and accurate selection of candidates, the need to educate and train these candidates, and the necessity to hold leaders accountable for their actions.

From Commander to Coach

If you were a child in the 1950s or before, you may remember a time when we looked to our elders and those in positions of authority with the utmost respect and awe. Strength and determination were characteristics to be respected. Our leaders were unquestioned and unapproachable.

Patients would go to their family doctor and follow his instructions to the letter, without understanding their health condition or illness. CEOs took the helm as commandeer and controller. Spiritual advisors were revered. The instructions of parents and teachers were followed out of respect for our elders.

Then came whirlwind technological advances, diverse cultural awareness in a global community, and the immediacy of new media - newspapers, magazines, television, radio, CDs and the Internet. We now know instantly how our leaders look and sound. We scrutinize and criticize how they move, the words they say, where they go at night, and how they dress. We have access to them through regular mail, e-mail, voice-mail, and fax.

Today's world is infinite in size and possibilities and requires a style that is dynamic and more coaching than dictatorial. We want to work with, not for, our leaders as we did in the past. Leaders must also be articulate, energetic, and empowering as well as experts at stress management and team-development.

We are re-examining the role and necessary skills of business managers, parents, and leaders in every field. The combination of management and leadership encompasses the human side of managing people in the workplace and the responsibility of motivating employees on an individual basis. Workshops to retrain upper management and future leaders in the new approach are being held across the country.

Marlene Tighe, independent communications consultant, was the area operations manager for Ohio Bell and then Ameritech for 38 years. She witnessed this transformation in leadership style firsthand, both in herself and in the other managers around her. She said in order to be highly competitive and successful, we must not lose sight of the human side of mentoring and leading. "The new governance for the workplace, and indeed society in general, requires a leadership style that is supportive and responsive to the full development of human potential," she said. "We need only to change 'our spirit of intent' and hold that space open to succeed in building growth, learning, and high performance in others."

As a leader who nurtured future leaders during the mid 1980s, Marlene promoted a transition in management from a supervisor/subordinate style to Harrison Owen's "open space" technique. A team approach was taken where managers were participants on projects, and subordinates had decision-making capabilities as well as accountability for the projects' outcome. Improved communication, listening, and people-reading skills were encouraged for both employees and customer relations.

The Opportunity to Lead

All the elements of a dynamic leader may exist in an individual, but those elements may never be revealed or utilized if the opportunity to lead does not occur. If too many leaders already are at the top of an organization, the organization does not recognize leader potential in a particular individual, or situations never occur which allow the leader to step forward and step ahead, leadership qualities will never become evident.

Some periods in history were more conducive to leadership promotion than other times. During the founding of our country, our nation witnessed the bravery of some of our most memorable leaders. The environment of declaration and assertion offered a prime opportunity for those with leadership ability such as George Washington, Alexander Hamilton, John Adams, and Thomas Jefferson.

Susan Coe Heitsch, Vice President of Corporate Affairs at Bank One, and recipient of the Leadership Award for Excellence in Management, pointed out that it's the responsibility of corporate managers to know and understand the potential of employees in order to utilize their capabilities. "Good leaders know what their people are made of," said Susan. "Often times we see someone we wouldn't have thought of as a "Joan of Arc," but that person is at the right time and the right place rising to the occasion, rising to the challenge."

Judy Chaffee, a self-employed contract trainer for Chrysler Corporation, said through her experience she has learned that if you allow people to do what they do best, everyone is successful. In addition to identifying subordinates' potential, managers also should not place them in a position to fail. Expecting an employee to perform a duty in which he is not capable of completing eliminates the possibility to triumph. "You can't put a square peg in a round hole," Judy said.

But many women believe their leadership potential is somewhat hampered by the demands of daily life. My sister, Margaret Cotterill, traffic manager for Cobra Electronics Corporation, added that women, in particular, are limited in their leadership opportunities because of family responsibilities. Caring for elderly parents, carting children to school, athletics, and piano, preparing meals, keeping house, doing laundry, and shopping for groceries continues to be "women's work" in most homes. She said these priorities of home and family consume time and energy leaving little for women to invest in a career.

In researching this book, I heard numerous concerns from women who are trying to balance career and family without having feelings of guilt draining them in both directions. In spite of this challenge, women are achieving higher levels then ever before. Throughout *MENTORING HEROES* you will be introduced to 52 incredible women I call "The Fabulous Fifty-Two." You may not recognize their names, but they are definitely leading the people around them. They are positively rippling the waters, making strides down paths few women have trod, blazing their own trails, and reaching heights higher than women before us dreamed possible. You also will meet the mentors who assisted these women in becoming leaders. These mentors are leaders who shared their time, knowledge, experience, and power of their rank to elevate their protégés to higher levels.

Leading a community from a distance has tremendous value. But mentoring, which is leading an individual to their highest potential, is so much more valuable and challenging. Leadership face-to-face requires the leader/mentor to leave their ego at the door. It is the giving and sharing of one person to another who may far exceed the giving mentor.

This book is a tribute to the leaders who shared themselves to mentor heroes, the leaders we look to guide us through life's challenges. My hope is that in relaying the experiences of The Fabulous Fifty-Two to you, your life might be touched by what you read. These dynamic women were positively influenced by a number of people in their lives. May their experiences positively influence you.

Chapter Two

MENTORING FOR SUCCESS

Mentors open doors. By sharing contacts, wisdom and experience, revealing destinies previously unforeseen, and accelerating the journeys to those destinations, mentors are catalysts in the development of future leaders and heroes.

Typically, when I interview men and ask if they are successful, they assess themselves in the context of their career. When I ask women if they are successful, they consider their personal relationships, friendships, cultural and social activities, contributions to the community, and children's welfare, as well as their professional achievements. For most women, success is a big picture encompassing many factors, not the culmination of a clear focused route to a high professional level.

A boss once told me all I had to do to be successful was to decide on my priorities and then keep them in order. At the time I was told this, I was a single parent with three children, working two jobs, and taking college classes toward a bachelor's degree. All positions were my priority. I certainly would never put my children's best interest after anyone else's. I had to work both jobs to pay our basic expenses. And I saw a college degree as a passage to a more lucrative future. There wasn't any way I could put one of those roles before the other.

My sister, Patti (Patricia) Doyle Brewer, told me to refer to her profession in this book as "Stockbroker slash Girl Scout Cookie Chairman." When she said that we laughed. But her humor is based in reality. She is more than a stockbroker. She is also wife, mother, sister, friend, daughter, elementary school volunteer, gardener, family entertainment director, and so on.

Women are multidimensional. And with this assortment of hats to wear, we have the possibility of encountering any number of mentors to help us in the many areas of our life. We don't have to meet the challenges of juggling these hats alone.

Three time Emmy Nominee and Golden Globe Award winning actress, singer, and motivational speaker, Ann Jillian, said she has had a number of mentors. The right person always has been there at the right time to help her. "My hat goes off to all those who mentored me," said Ann. "Those lovely people built me, built my self esteem, layer upon layer."

Anna Cheng Catalano, Senior Vice President, of Sales Operations for BP Amoco Oil Company, said she had many different mentors during her career who helped her at different times. Mentors introduced her to people she might otherwise have been bashful to introduce herself. They assessed her skills and weaknesses and helped her career to skyrocket. Anna said mentors open doors. Once inside those doors, you are on your own. You must prove you deserve to be there.

Sister Mary Stella Schellenberger said the fact that

women hold so many low paying jobs in fields such as child care, elder care, nursing, and teaching, shows that women base success on personal satisfaction of doing something to raise humanity with love rather than on acquiring a higher income. We certainly appreciate a little money in the bank after paying the bills, but the paycheck isn't the main reason we work, she said.

Jeannette B. Martens Sorrentino, DDS said currently success for her is being able to balance working part-time as a dentist and caring for her three daughters. She has invested many years in education and experience toward her dental career. This investment in her profession is very important to her but no less important than the welfare of her daughters. "I don't measure success in terms of purely money. I didn't have my children to prove biologically I could have them. I want to raise them," said Jeannette.

Both of my grandmothers worked outside of the home, which was not uncommon during the 1930s and 40s when my parents were growing up. Many women worked during World War II. But most mothers of the 1950s did not. They were full-time, at-home moms. These women raised their daughters to be wives and mothers. Therefore, it was not uncommon for those of us who had to work while raising our families, to receive more understanding from our grandmothers than our mothers.

Initially, when I returned to the work force, I had few marketable skills to offer a perspective employer. I had to raise my level of experience and knowledge before I could be financially independent. Getting that extra education and training while working and caring for my family was very challenging. Because I do not want my daughters, Lisa and Erin, to struggle as I had, I stress the necessity for them to be emotionally and financially independent. Obtaining a college degree was never a question but a requirement in their lives. I believe education is a key element that enables their dream for their future to become a reality. It offers more opportunity for life-style options and choices.

But as is usually the way, once we think we have something all figured out, a new twist comes into the picture. I am now coming across young women in their twenties and thirties prepared professionally to face the world independently but struggling to balance career and family to their expectations. That element of guilt seems most prevalent in women with children. We are very conscious of the other people with whom we share this planet, especially those who are near and dear to us. No matter how we live, we do not lose sight of the personal connections we feel and our obligation to nurture.

Women deal with pregnancy, care for the home, and have the main responsibility of raising children. And most of us wouldn't have it any other way. But how can we personally offer our children the optimum level of love and care we want for them and reach our own optimum level professionally after investing time and money in our education without feeling as if neither our children or ourselves are being cheated?

For a number of years, I was a full-time, at-home mom and still went to bed every night feeling guilty. I always felt I should have spent more time with one child or another, my husband, the house, other family members, or friends. So, of course when I was working outside the home, this guilt increased. At this point in my life I'm beginning to see a much broader picture. My children are 23, 20, and 18 years old. They are becoming more and more independent, leaving me with more time to devote to my writing.

For me, success is seeing these children growing into beautiful, responsible, compassionate, and independent young adults; finally enjoying a marriage that is mature, respectful, loving, and fun; reaching out to family, friends, and the people around me; building a writing career in my way at my pace; and pursuing intellectual, spiritual, and cultural interests. I've finally realized all my dreams can and will come true - at different times of my life and with a little help from other people who know more than I at the time. Having mentors to rely on for guidance, support, and inspiration will make all the difference in reaching my greatest potential.

Customized Mentoring

With the diversity of roles a woman plays in each period of her life, comes the opportunity to learn from many different mentors in many different ways. Linaya Hahn, LNC is an educator and public speaker on Premenstrual Syndrome and the founder of the PMS Holistic Center. She is the author of *PMS: Solving the Puzzle*. She works with physicians in distributing information on PMS. Linaya said she had used a number of mentors for different information on PMS but would have preferred to have one primary mentor who offered opportunity for clear direction as well as expertise. "I'd work with one person on progesterone, another for sleep disorders, someone else for information on full spectrum light, and then piece all this together. If I could have found one solid mentor on PMS, I probably would have gotten where I am a lot faster," said Linaya.

There are as many variations of mentoring as there are people on the planet. As you will learn from the stories of The Fabulous Fifty-Two, any variation can work. After all, if we as women have to juggle numerous facets of our lives, the mentoring and being mentored also has to be juggled. The relationship should be customized to the protégé's needs and the generosity of the mentor.

Ingrid Sharos is Supervisor of Adult Probation in DuPage County, Illinois. She has had a number of mentors and role models. She has learned from them and grown at a faster rate because of them. But Ingrid says mentors aren't images to duplicate. The protégé should develop in their own way at their own pace. "Each individual is responsible for their own direction," said Ingrid.

The mentoring relationship can be to enhance any area of your life or combination of areas. For example, your pastor or rabbi may advise you spiritually, your athletic trainer assists you with your physical development, your stockbroker guides you financially, and an elderly neighbor may be a tremendous help with parenting issues. Or perhaps it is your religious leader who guides you in finances, your athletic trainer in spirituality, your stockbroker in parenting, and so forth.

Most mentors come and go as needed. They share what they know, who they know, and how to get wherever. Mentors also gain in the relationship. They have the potential to learn, grow, and gain new friendships through the course of mentoring. As teachers often testify, teachers learn from the students, as well as the other way around.

A mentoring relationship can be structured or unstructured. Mentors and protégés can be randomly assigned or carefully paired. There may even be designated guidelines to follow and activities to accomplish. The relationship might also be very informal. The relationship may form after a request from a protégé, or as a result of living or working in close proximity. Meetings can be called as the need arises rather than at set time intervals.

A mentor may play a significant role in your life for a specific period of time. The experience can be a launching pad for you in an area you have had little experience. For example, you may have been hired for your first job in sales. Your manager supports and advises you through the initial period. Once you are capable of maintaining your accounts, as well as attract new clients, you may no longer need ongoing input from the mentor.

On the other hand, this mentor might be so knowledgeable you continue to seek her advice and direction throughout your career. For the entire time you are at that company, this manager is there for you. The manager, or you, may even move on to another company, and your relationship continues.

Occasionally a special mentor crosses our path momentarily, as if we met purely to receive their message. We may know this person casually, or not at all, but they say something to us that is the essence of mentoring. You may strike up a conversation with this person in the checkout line at a grocery store or the doctor's waiting room, and the few words they offer shine a light at the end of a tunnel you thought would never end.

About eight years ago, I was going though my first divorce after being married sixteen years. I was talking with a casual friend - actually, I was crying - and said that I was feeling overwhelmed and could not handle the emotional, physical, and financial responsibility of my children alone. My friend responded that I was crying for no reason. I *was* handling everything. My children were doing wonderfully. They were strong, healthy, and happy. My bills were paid. I was growing intellectually and professionally. I was making great strides in improving my life. I stopped, thought, and realized what my friend said was true. Those few words were a pivotal point for me in self-confidence.

Until the invention of the automobile, people lived and worked lifetimes in one location. Everyone in the entire community was your neighbor. If you wanted to be a seamstress, hairdresser, teacher, or midwife, you went for guidance to the expert, interned under that person, and took their place when they retired. That expert may have been a relative - parent, uncle, whatever. But you knew that expert and they knew you, which made it very easy to strike up a mentoring relationship.

As we become more and more mobile, our roots become longer, twisting and turning from town-to-town and state-to-state. Today we bring our children to see their grandparents on holidays instead of every other Sunday. Our regular doctor is really a group of physicians who do not recognize us outside the office. And we don't live in the same town long enough for our hairdresser to see our roots grow out.

Prior to conglomerates, takeovers, and downsizing, even if we didn't live in the same location forever, we used to at least work for the same company until retirement. My father, John Doyle, worked for Illinois Bell Telephone Company for thirty years. He had the same superiors to go to for guidance most of his career and a number of subordinates who counted on him. That was typical then. Companies were loyal to employees and vice versa.

Growing up surrounded by people you know on a personal level, or working for the same company your entire career, rarely happens anymore. So how do we find a candidate for mentor or convince that person to mentor us? The advantage of a global society is that everyone on the planet is our neighbor. Maybe we don't know them since childhood, but with a little observation we can identify a perspective mentor, approach that person, and ask if they would consider assisting in our development.

Most people I've contacted over the years to request an interview have agreed to talk with me. After all, what can be more flattering than to have someone value us and eager to learn from our knowledge and experience? Mentoring is much the same way. A protégé consults a mentor because that person is respected and admired for the level of wisdom and success attained. The mentor's power is evident, and the protégé is humbly requesting the mentor to share their insight.

Sharing Your Expertise

For every four or five wonderful stories about a mentor, I have heard one "off the record" about a woman who either refused to help someone or deliberately stood in someone's way. There are women who are obstructing other women's progress. This doesn't make any sense to me. We complain that women are making only about 75% of what men are making in the same position, and that the opportunity to advance is limited. We know that so many women, single, married, with, and without children are struggling financially. So why are we women prohibiting ourselves from advancement?

If your friend jumped over a cliff, would you? Remember your parents asking you such a question? We teach our children to look at what others are doing and think for themselves, but how can they think for themselves if the information isn't being shared? We refer to this period in time as the information age. We know knowledge is power. We see information available on an international basis, yet as women, we are not readily passing on what we know to other women. We are not passing on the power.

It seems that women are more generous to other women in female dominated areas such as nursing, parenting, homemaking, and hairdressing. Women are basically caretakers. Most of the time, we share recipes, child-care tips, cosmetic expertise, and marital suggestions. Perhaps we feel secure in leadership roles in these fields, having held them for generations. We don't feel threatened in seeing another woman advance in those roles where we are confident in our abilities to retain our own space.

Such sharing is not readily available in fields newly opened to women such as senior management positions in business and the military. From 1988 to 1992 Janet Faye Damm was in the U. S. Navy. As a Yeoman E-4, she found the higher ranking females to be the most challenging with whom to work. "Maybe it was the competition, or not wanting to be viewed as weak, or wanting to act harder in a male world," said Janet, "but for the most part, women in the Navy were not good to each other."

First Vice President of Solomon Smith Barney, Inc., Sue (Susan) Darby, had a number of mentors. Many were men, and one of her very favorite mentors was a woman, but Sue said she did have trouble with some women, particularly at the beginning of her career as a stockbroker. "There have been women along the line who said they did it the hard way so I could, too," said Sue. "For heavens sake! Let's be proud of what we know and share it."

I have heard a number of reasons why women don't, can't, or won't mentor. We do tend to be overworked and wear more hats than we can handle. We also like the attention. Being the sole woman in the forefront certainly puts us in the spotlight. Also, women are just beginning to hold high-ranking positions in business, and therefore are insecure about our own stability.

Some of this lack of support is also due to being stuck in a consciousness of scarcity. If there is one pie, and I keep slicing pieces and giving them away, there is less for me. But abundance doesn't work that way. It's really just the opposite. In order to receive, we must give. And the more we give, the more we will receive.

Also, the giving and receiving are not identical but rather in regards to giving what is needed and receiving what we need. If you give someone who is homeless $10 for lunch, you don't need that person to return the $10. However, someday you may need something from another person, such as an opportunity to work in a particular company. Hopefully, that person will help you with what you need rather than return exactly what you had given away.

Nancy Wilson Dickey, MD, President of the American Medical Association, and family physician, said women have to stop acting as roadblocks and wrecking balls toward other women in the same field. She said it is our responsibility to mentor. "I do think we all, particularly women, have an overt responsibility to mentor," said Nancy. "I realize mentoring is an extra burden on an already overflowing plate, but we need more active mentoring. We are clearly, as a gender and society, redesigning roles. Any period of redefinition requires the open sharing of pros and cons, wins and losses, and mountains and valleys so each one of us doesn't have to experience these things."

The October 1997 *CBA Record*, the Chicago Bar Association's journal for attorneys, focused on the importance of mentoring in the legal profession. In her plea to fellow attorneys to share knowledge with less experienced attorneys, Patricia C. Bobb writes in her editorial on the President's Page that young lawyers learning from the more experienced ones is the greatest tradition of their profession. She explains the decline in mentoring is due to the pressure to bring in more business to increase billable hours. Building the firm financially is taking precedence over building the profession.

Vicky (Victoria) Bush-Joseph, JD is an attorney and partner in the firm Bush-Joseph & Horwich. She said she would have loved to have had an older and wiser female mentor in which to identify and go to for advice, especially in regards to handling home and career effectively. Her mother was a nurse but didn't work full time when Vicky was a child. Not many women in her neighborhood worked outside the home. Vicky was one of the few women attorneys at the time, and the more experienced female attorneys were unavailable to her when she started practicing law in 1982. "The older female attorneys weren't very nurturing. I guess they felt if they did it on their own, I could, too," said Vicky.

Vicky tries to do as much mentoring as she possibly can. She has a full schedule as wife, mother of two young children, and attorney. Making the time to mentor is difficult but important to her, because she knows how much easier her life would have been had there been another woman attorney for her to talk to in the early part of her career.

In order to bond and have access to upper management, Marcia E. Balestri, geochemist and vice president of the Environmental Technology Development Group at TRW, Inc. said she had to be one of the boys. "It's a cultural thing after a long day in the field to go for a beer. I don't have any problem fitting in with the guys sharing war stories and wisdom. That's where I learned a lot and got a lot of information," said Marcia. But she added she would have liked to have had female mentors, too. "Sometimes it was a little uncomfortable talking with men about certain issues," she said.

Employees interested in solid business direction often approach Susan Schreter, President and Cofounder of Caring Products, International, Inc., a publicly traded marketer of cost-effective absorbent products. At 36 years of age, Susan is running her second manufacturing business. She said she is obligated to helping people who seek her advice, and especially women in starting their own companies. Most women have not been exposed to the skills they need, such as how to go for banking, financing, developing a product from scratch, and managing distribution. Susan said she has been lucky to have had a top education and enjoys passing on what she knows.

According to the June 25, 1997 Journal of American Medical Association, people with a large circle of friends get sick less and have a better sense of self-worth. On the other hand, a weak social network is associated with higher rates of depression and other forms of psychological distress. These people also tend to have less resistance to infection. So perhaps the social benefit of mentoring may even contribute to better physical health as well as personal and professional development.

If there is but little water in the stream, it is the fault, not of the channel, but of the source.

Saint Jerome
Letter 17

Chapter Three

STRUCTURED
MENTORING PROGRAMS

Business, education, medicine, psychology, athletics, the arts, religion - even self-esteem. Structured mentoring programs can be found in almost any category you can imagine. And although the programs are structured, the structures vary so much it would be difficult to find two that are identical.

There are programs for teens, women, families, entrepreneurs, college students, and elementary students. Programs are sponsored by schools, hospitals, businesses, professional organizations, churches, and individuals. Some meet weekly. Some meet bi-weekly. Some meet as often as the paired mentor and protégé decide upon. One program mentioned in this chapter actually meets only once a year.

If you want to be a mentor or be mentored, look around your community. You will be surprised how many mentors and protégés you easily will find. Mentoring groups are advertised on the radio, television, and in print ads. Nearly every one of The Fabulous Fifty-Two have encountered or participated in a structured mentoring program. Chances are, you have, too.

Many participants of structured programs said they preferred personally selecting a mentor on their own, although they wouldn't eliminate the structured programs. All forms of mentoring are beneficial on some level. The vast number of programs available indicates that structured or unstructured, mentoring works.

Adolescent Development with a Mentor

Theresa McNally, Ed.D., psychotherapist, conducted a study on the mentor-protégé relationship for her doctoral thesis. The study was done in 1986 at a junior boys boarding school. Theresa compared twelve 14 to 15 years old ninth grade boys with mentors to a control group of boys the same age who did not have mentors. To begin with, Theresa discovered which students had a mentoring relationship with a teacher already established prior to her arrival. Once these relationships were determined, she observed and questioned these partnerships for two years.

According to Theresa, the boys with mentors appeared to have more power than the typical students of the same age without mentors. They took on more leadership roles in regards to decision making and initiating change at the school. Theresa said it was as if the boys with mentors aligned their power with their teachers.

She also made some discoveries she hadn't anticipated. She was surprised at the satisfaction the teachers received from mentoring and their natural ability to mentor on a number of levels - emotional, career, academic, social, and family. She was surprised at the amount of extra work the mentored students took on for their teachers, such as grading papers and helping in the classroom. Most of all, Theresa was surprised at how much the boys developed psychologically over that time period.

The study was motivated by Theresa's interest in the benefits of the mentoring experience in adult males and she wanted to know if those benefits would occur in adolescent boys. She said she had not experienced such a relationship personally and didn't think such opportunities were as readily available for women as they were for men. "I was enormously jealous of men I knew who had mentors. Mentors had played huge roles in these men's lives. I yearned for such a relationship," Theresa said.

Career Links is a program that does offer opportunities for teen-aged girls to experience the mentoring relationship and to expose them to the working world. It is an eleven-year-old division of a nonprofit, award winning program in Chicago called Women Employed. Women Employed focuses on expanding career opportunities for women. This program has assisted more than 30,000 women over the past 25 years.

Career Links' mentoring groups meet 90 minutes every other week. Groups are informal, mixing at will, in ratios of approximately two mentors to every three teens. Conversation is lively and continuous and centers on career exploration, employability skills, verbal and nonverbal communications, and goal-setting.

Career Links mentors are a powerful army which empowers the young women-to-be. They are committed to the young women, making it clear that as volunteers, they are there because they choose to be. Nearly 500 professional women makeup this diverse group of volunteers. Mentors are carefully interviewed and screened. Once accepted, they are instructed as to how to present careers and the skills and education necessary to enter highlighted professions. The mentors are trained in how to identify abuse, stress, and other challenging situations faced by the teens. They also are informed as to which staff member they should refer the teens for additional assistance.

Mentors are trained to meet the young protégés where they are and not where the mentor would like them to be. Program Director Linda Shepard offered this example, "occasionally one of the brightest and best teens begins to gain weight, and it's evident she is pregnant. Mentors can't help but be affected by that, first feeling anger and then hopelessness, wondering where they had failed. Then they come back to accepting the teen and her decisions," Linda said.

"These girls want to go college. They have the desire to live with integrity. They have energy, enthusiasm, dreams, and blind faith to think, if you give them a chance, they can make it. They want a good life. But they have no resources and no clue how to get it," said Linda. "Career Links offers an introduction to successful role models, answers, and another way to be in life."

There has been no tracking system to monitor the growth of the teens, but Linda said the women and teens love Career Links. Most come back year after year in spite of many challenges. At one point, the location for meetings had to be changed due to the growing number of members and the gang violence near the facility. A bus was provided to transport the teens from the original location to the new site. This change of location meant the young women had to come out in the evenings leaving their homes and televisions, go past the gangs and drugs, and commute longer to get there.

The protégés' determination to meet with mentors shows the desire they have to open themselves to new ideas and a new way of life. Linda said the transformation the teens make in Career Links is evident. They come into the program from a hard core community using bad language. They are chronic truants, runaways, and opposing gang members. Some of the teens have children and may or may not be in touch with the father. Many of their parents are in jail.

Yet after only a few meetings, the teens put their gang differences aside. They begin mimicking their mentors' dress, actions, and language. They open up their thoughts and hearts to the mentors, trusting in them and appreciating the attention showered on them. "What happens in this program is miraculous," said Linda. "There is mutual respect between the mentors and teens. And the process of growth is reciprocal."

Fourteen years ago in another Chicago area mentoring program, Jane Hayden, Director of Traffic at WGN Television, met protégé Darius Stinson. At that time, Darius was a nine-year-old boy living with his single mother in the Cabrini Green Housing Project. Jane's goal was to offer a role model and mentor outside of the people with whom Darius came in contact in his neighborhood. "I wanted to be a part of his life and someone he could depend on all of his life," said Jane.

Like the mentors in Career Links, Jane had to learn how to offer Darius choices without imposing her own choices on him. She also learned to appreciate him for whom he was, not whom she thought he should be. "He lived in another world," said Jane. "It wasn't safe to stand in front of his apartment building or to walk on certain floors. He didn't ask, 'What should I wear today?' or 'What should I eat?' but "What is clean to wear?' and 'Is there anything to eat?" she said.

From the beginning of this relationship, Jane said she was accepted as a part of Darius' family and he a part of hers. When Darius was younger, his mother would tease

Jane by calling Darius her son when he was doing something good but Jane's son when he was bad. For the most part, though, Darius did very well with the extra attention and guidance of a mentor. His grades in school were above average and he was chosen captain of the football team in high school.

Jane said she thought she had done a pretty good job helping Darius along the way until he graduated from high school and got into some trouble. As we all learn as parents, Jane discovered guidance is needed on a life-long basis. "I had thought my part was done. Apparently, it's never done," she said.

With support from Darius' family and Jane, Darius is on the right track again. He is working full time and supporting his girlfriend and two children.

Jane has started another mentoring program in the area. More than half of the mentors are WGN employees, and the rest are friends. These mentors joined the program because they witnessed the positive results of mentoring through Jane's experience with Darius and wished to do the same.

The group meets one-on-one with elementary school students after school until 7 PM. Mentors help the children with homework and life issues. The program is in its fourth year and several mentor-protégé relationships have continued year to year.

Monique Anawis, MD., Eye Physician and Surgeon and Director of Ophthalmology Teaching at University of Chicago Hospitals, has been involved with several different mentoring programs. While in college, Monique was a member of the Big Sisters program, and later a program called Horizons. Both are aimed at pairing young adults with inner city children to expose them to a mature, healthy, and balanced role model in which to relate.

Monique also has talked to young athletes and coaches

at the Olympic Training Center in Milwaukee, Wisconsin, because she was an ice skater during her elementary and high school years. She tells of her own experiences and how her athletic training helps her even today as an eye physician and surgeon. Learning how to travel, communicate with all different types of people, compete with confidence and courage, persevere, visualize, and set goals are not just skills she used as an athlete but also uses today in her medical practice. By sharing her experiences, Monique gives her audience someone with whom they can identify and the encouragement to attain reachable goals.

Mentoring the Student

Education doesn't guarantee a more prosperous or happier future, but it offers opportunities otherwise unavailable. Data collected in March of 1995 and reported in the CAM Report stated that the average annual income without a high school diploma to be $13,697, with a high school diploma to be $20,248, with a Bachelor's degree to be $37,224, and with a Master's degree to be $46,332. The more education a student receives, the more choices she has in the job market and likelihood she is to be financially independent.

When you mentor a student you are telling them you believe in them and the significance of education. Students are more likely to succeed with the extra support and attention. And that makes good business sense because unemployment decreases with higher education. The price of mentoring a student is far less than the tax burden of long-term public financial assistance. And as described in the "Ripple Effect," everyone who excels has the potential to raise the people around her. You are not just mentors leading one person to a better future but their family, friends, and neighbors as well.

I started college when I was 33 years old. The Parent Teacher Organization at my children's school in Roselle, Illinois awarded me a scholarship, which I greatly needed at that time. When I accepted the scholarship I thanked the Waterbury School PTO on behalf of myself and my children, because by helping me raise my earning potential through education, I would be better able to provide for my children's needs and assist them with their educational expenses.

Corporate America and smaller businesses across the country recognize this responsibility to support education through mentoring. Most encourage employees to mentor in person, but there are many variations in this technological age. Hewlett Packard Employees mentor via e-mail. The one-to-one relationships motivate 5-12th grade students to excel in academics as well as communication and problem solving skills.

Throughout the Chicago area businesses are encouraging employees to leave their positions for about one hour a week to mentor elementary school students. Schools usually match students in need of extra tutoring or attention with mentor candidates. Mentors review material learned in class, read aloud to the students, and listen to the children read.

The cost of mentoring varies from company to company. Some employers suggest employees donate their time after work hours. Some allow time off during work hours but without pay or commission. And some employers offer the employees the time off with pay.

WITS, Working In The Schools, is a non-profit organization which screens, trains, and places Chicago employees and retirees who volunteer to tutor with public elementary school students. During the 1996-97 school year WITS donated more than 30,000 hours by mentoring a half day every other week.

After school mentoring programs in the Chicago area can be found through the Tutor-Mentor Connection. This organization is a non-profit tutoring network. It publishes a directory of more than 300 sites. Directories are available in schools, libraries and city businesses.

Mentoring is at least as important in higher education as in elementary and high school. No longer is there a typical college student. In addition to the incoming high school graduate, universities are filling classrooms with returning adults of all ages and situations. Women are returning to college after raising families. Employees are required to attain a bachelor degree to retain current positions. Professionals are considering career changes and need the education to make the switch.

Recognizing that students cannot focus their undivided attention on studies, high schools and most colleges and universities offer peer and/or alumni mentoring to students. Balancing the many aspects of life in addition to the responsibilities involved in going to school - attending classes, studying, and completing homework - is complicated and stressful. Having a mentor on which to rely for advice, friendship, and support often makes the difference in sailing the high seas or giving up the ship before the sails are set.

Educational institutions offer a wide range of programs. Several programs match students with faculty members according to discipline. Faculty members/mentors are available for guidance throughout the students' attendance at that school.

In another program, the Chicago Alliance for Minority Participation, which is a part of a nationwide consortium of colleges and universities, the focus is on minorities. The consortium's goal is to have mentors encourage more minorities to attain college degrees.

In the Medical Student Mentorship Program at the University of Chicago Hospitals, experienced physicians are paired with students. Cardiologist Amy Coene Bales, M.D. participates as a mentor in the program. Her protégé is seeking advice as to how to balance the many demands in her daily life while attending medical school. Amy's own challenge of balancing responsibilities of wife, mother, and doctor makes finding opportunities to meet with her protégé challenging. Amy said getting together with her protégé is difficult because of both of their schedules. Their solution is to 'talk' through e-mail.

Cheryl Conover, Ph.D. is the Professor of Medicine, Director of the Endocrine Research Unit, and Vice Chair for Research in the Department of Medicine at the Mayo Clinic in Rochester, Minnesota. Cheryl said she understands that the time factor in most women's lives in the medical field makes it nearly impossible to find the opportunity to mentor. There is the pressure to seek more grants and see more patients during work time while tending to so many family and social responsibilities that little time is left for mentoring. However, Mayo does host a high school mentoring program that Cheryl finds manageable and is showing some very positive results.

Students are carefully screened and then offered basic summer jobs at Mayo with the intention of exposing these students to the activities and personnel at the clinic. Many students return summer after summer gaining insight and offering Mayo staff some extra assistance. Cheryl said the students are bright and enthusiastic. "They have so much passion and compassion," she said.

One student Cheryl originally hired for a mundane job returned for employment at Mayo several summers in a row. Cheryl found she could call on her protégé for challenging, independent projects. Cheryl finally hired the student as a full-time technician over someone more experienced. "I discovered she was a star. She not only performed incredibly, she was so good, she first-authored a paper in a major journal and gave an oral presentation to the National Endocrine Society," said Cheryl. That student is now in medical school and continues to keep in contact with Cheryl.

An alternative therapy called Guided Imagery and Music is designed with mentoring as an integral part of the program. GIM is a technique using music to induce an altered state of mind. Once in this state, the images experienced are shared with the guide to facilitate a holistic approach to healing, growth, and transformation.

GIM therapists must complete an intensive three-year program of study for accreditation. Interns are required to report their sessions to their mentor but can access their assigned mentor, or any other experienced mentor in the program, any time questions arise. GIM board certified music therapist Louise Dimiceli-Mitran, MT-BC said that having a mentor with which to consult after sessions is a necessity because of GIM's unpredictability. "Nothing is cut and dry in GIM. There is no set process to follow. GIM is a client-centered therapy. Therapists can't anticipate what they will encounter from the subconscious," said Louise.

GIM developer and The Bonny Foundation director, instructor, and lecturer Helen L. Bonny, Ph.D., R.M.T. said mentoring is important for the guide/therapist to understand the effect of their work and for necessary advice. It is not just an intellectual process. GIM involves the whole person - body, mind, and spirit. Each session takes considerable amount of energy and time, and the mentor plays a key role in the therapist's ability to guide her own transformation and also the client's.

Kathy Ballman is an adolescent counselor at Lancaster High School and a domestic violence counselor at a shelter in California. She also is a student in the graduate degree program at Prescott College in Arizona but only attends classes on campus for one four day period each year. The majority of her classes are conducted in the workplace.

Kathy's entire graduate degree program is linked to mentoring. She begins each course by seeking a mentor to teach her about an aspect of the field for a designated period of time. She proposes a curriculum to the college and the mentor, and once approved, works and studies under that mentor on their job site. Mentors assign homework, correct assignments, administer exams, and report grades to the college. Kathy's major is in counseling, so studies focus on community awareness, crisis intervention, and youth programs. She participates on forums and assists at domestic violence shelters as part of her studies.

Teacher/mentors receive token salaries and some extra help from Kathy as she learns about the responsibilities of the position she is assigned. Many offer her paid positions after completion of the course. Mentors also assist Kathy with networking and finding other mentors or areas of study to further her education.

Kathy said the program works because it offers a realistic view of her choice of career rather than a textbook example that does not apply. The program is very creative and can be molded to fit the society in which she lives. Kathy said she gained "leaps and bounds," receiving so much more than she hoped from her mentors. She has an accurate picture of what to expect after graduation and what she needs to know to be employable.

Mentoring Church to Church

Sandy Oler is an active church volunteer. She volunteers many hours each week to meet the needs of her church, Fox Valley Christian, and its congregation. But not only do individuals volunteer within a church, churches volunteer to assist other growing churches in programs called scaffolding.

Recently Sandy participated in an outreach program to mentor a new church, West Ridge Community. This church-to-church mentoring directs, advises, and handholds volunteers of the new church through its infancy. Fox Valley Christian Church acted as West Ridge's big brother, or mentor, until West Ridge's own leadership was strong enough to take over.

Professional Development

Women often find themselves in need of or desire for higher education and an employment change, but our success can be held back by self-doubt. A mentor can ease a protégé through that transition and into financial and emotional independence.

South West Women Working Together helps academically and economically disadvantaged women on the southwest side of Chicago. This incredible organization mentors the whole woman. Their goal is to discourage minimum wage paying jobs and encourage personal development and self-empowerment. The women ultimately have the ability to obtain and hold substantial jobs in order to support their family without government assistance. South West Women Working Together sees the women through the entire process from beginning to end, guiding them through employment training, educational degree or certification, job interviews, and finally, settled into a career.

The publicly funded agency offers counseling and instruction on building self-esteem, budgeting, communication skills, and managing conflicts. It also supplies support services such as child-care, medical care, housing, and transportation for women enrolled in an academic program. It even dresses the women for job interviews from shoes to cologne.

In another program sponsored by the Joliet Will County Center for Economic Development and Small Business Development Center, successful business owners are paired with new business owners. After completing questionnaires and the first few initial meetings, mentors and protégés meet monthly in the year-long program. The volunteer mentors also are available throughout the month to answer business questions and offer guidance.

Laurie Scordo, founder of Laurel Gifts, a mail order business which features customized gourmet gift baskets for all occasions, is a participant in the program. She said she has developed a friendship with her mentor and her business has grown substantially, in part, because of the experience. Laurie said her mentor gave her some solid direction based on her goals. She gave her feedback and intelligent, experienced advice.

About six years ago, The Honorable Robert K. Kilander, the director of the Judicial Education Committee, instituted a two-part mentoring program for judges in the DuPage County judicial system. Previously to the mentoring program, judges were like islands. Judge Kilander said he noticed a lack of continuity and cohesiveness among the judges. That situation isn't happening as much any more, partly because of the mentoring program.

The first part of the mentoring program consists of a reference-type handbook. The book offers advice on easing the transition from attorney to judge. Here judges can find suggestions on how to wrap up their law practice and also procedures to consider as an associate judge.

The second part is the actual mentoring program. Circuit Court judges are paired with one or more incoming associate judges. The mentor/circuit court judge acts as a go-between for judicial business at meetings representing the concerns of the associate judge. The mentor also is a source of experience and wisdom to access when questions arise.

Circuit Court Judge, The Honorable Hollis L. Webster, has been on both sides of the judicial mentoring fence. "It's invaluable for anyone to be the benefactor of a mentor," she said.

Hollis added that, although she wouldn't do away with the judicial mentoring program, structured mentoring does have its drawbacks. When relationships are randomly selected, protégés might not recognize or wish to emulate the qualities and characteristics of the mentor. Also, mentors might not have the additional experience or knowledge to raise the level of expertise of the associate judge.

Hollis was recently assigned to mentor a judge who is fifteen years older and, in some ways, more experienced than she is. She said she is very happy to mentor the judge. He is a wonderful man, but she does not feel he really needs her guidance.

Hollis added that the most effective relationship occurs when respect, chemistry, and admiration exists before pairing up for mentoring. Perhaps those elements were not existent in the relationship Hollis described, but she said they can, and do, exist in other DuPage County judicial mentoring relationships.

Where I was born and where and how
I have lived is unimportant. It is what
I have done with where I have been
that should be of interest.

Georgia O'Keeffe (1976)

Chapter Four

MIRRORING OUR
ROLE MODELS

Finding a role model is easier than finding a mentor.
Role models are neighbors, coworkers, bosses,
relatives, religious leaders, politicians, and
television personalities. They are people with whom we
have limited or no direct communication. They are not
available to question or seek one-on-one advice. We learn
from role models by listening to their words and analyzing
their actions.

A role model may be a woman who lives down the street
from you. You admire the way she relates to her children
and how they respond to her. Or maybe this role model is
a boss who includes his subordinates in decision-making
and values their productivity. Perhaps your role model is
your state representative who seems to truly care about
the people he represents. Any one or all of these people
can be your role models. You look to each of them in a

different way for guidance in a different part of your life.

Janet Faye Damm, Credit Analyst for Ford Motor Credit Company and past Navy Yeoman, is only 27 years old but has lived in Illinois, Kentucky, Hawaii, California, and Texas. As a result of her mobile life-style, or perhaps because of an inborn characteristic, she said she often studies people around her. There are always students, friends, and coworkers from whom she can watch and learn.

If you want to be an attorney, gourmet chef, airline pilot, or dancer, you can study the great leaders of the past and present. You can learn from their experiences and how they reacted to the roller coaster of their lives. Following a personality is easier today then ever before. The potential role model doesn't have to be in your face. If potential role models are physically distant and you can't witness their daily activities first hand, you can read about them in encyclopedias, newspapers, journals, books, the Internet or view them on video or television.

I receive a great deal of information to write about from interviewing people, so I am always interested in television talk shows where people are interviewed on the air. I look to Oprah Winfrey and Barbara Walters as role models. I respect their persistent yet compassionate approach in gathering information. I also appreciate their intent. They don't ask intrusive questions unless the questions are pertinent to the story.

I can learn from these women by studying their television interviews. I can read about them in newspaper and magazine articles and study who they are and why they do what they do. So even though I do not have access to them to consult with them or be advised by them firsthand, I can learn from them by watching and listening.

Margaret Cotterill, traffic manager for Cobra Electronics Corporation, said she looked to the late Cardinal Joseph Bernadine as a role model. From what she had seen of him on television and read about him in newspapers, she said he offered an example of leadership that was gentle, compassionate, and inspiring to not only those in the Catholic Church he was appointed to direct, but everyone who knew him. Margaret said Cardinal Bernadine motivated people to be the best they could be. People believed in him and willingly followed his example. He was a model of the type of person Margaret would like to be personally and professionally as a leader.

Radiating in the Spotlight

Most of us don't make television appearances before large audiences or preach before a congregation, but it is important to remember that we are always being watched. We are in contact with people everyday in our homes, our communities, our work, and our spiritual and cultural activities. These people are observing us. We are teaching others how to be a boss by the way we treat our subordinates. We teach our children about relationships by the way we interact with our spouse, siblings, parents, and friends.

For some reason, it seems we can do a hundred wonderful things for our children, but the one time we slip up, they remember that incident and remind us about it for the rest of our lives. One time I forgot to pick up my daughter, Erin, from work. She was 16 years old at the time, and I had picked her up from school, her friends' homes, Girl Scouts, ballet, band practice, and Catechism classes hundreds of times before. The one time I forgot her, it was as if I permanently had broken her heart and trust in me. That was four years ago, and she still reminds me of that day.

In a sense, we are on center stage most of our lives.

Someone is watching and listening to our words and actions more often than we are aware. Unfortunately, as in the story with Erin, our mistakes are remembered more often than our achievements. This factor presents us with tremendous responsibility. I pray daily that everything I say and do is done with love and wisdom. I feel with those intentions, jealousy, anger, and the other negatives that get in the way will remain in check, and that most of the time my thoughts and actions will be productive and empowering for me and others.

Sue (Susan) M. Holstein, Ph.D., licensed clinical psychologist and hypnotherapist, said she is very conscious of her actions because she often sees others watching her. Sue said she realizes her secretary, Nancy, follows her lead in relation to clients and must have no doubt how to handle situations on Sue's behalf in the interim between initial client contact and their appointment with Sue. Nancy treats clients as Sue would treat them. Sue said Nancy is compassionate and intuitive. She models Sue's client approach and represents Sue in her absence.

Parents as Role Models

Harriet Gerber Lewis, Chairman of the Board, Gerber Plumbing Fixtures, Corp., a plumbing fixtures manufacturer, assumed the lead at Gerber in 1953 when her father, Max Gerber, died. At the time Harriet was married and the mother of three children. She had never been involved in the company's day-to-day activities or been in business before. The plumbing and manufacturing businesses were highly competitive and very male-dominated environments. However, Harriet did have a bachelor's degree from Northwestern University and had watched her father build Gerber Plumbing Fixtures since its founding in 1932. She has since taken the company's annual sales volume from $7.5 million to more than $114 million. It's not unusual for a parent to mentor their children. You will read stories from members of The Fabulous Fifty-Two in the following chapters who learned a great deal from their parents. But Harriet's situation was a little different in that, by the time she was involved directly in Gerber Plumbing Fixtures, her father was not physically available to her. Harriet did not have her father to ask advice or introduce her to key distributors or other business contacts when she took over the company. Her father was a role model, though, because she had witnessed his expertise first hand and drew on past circumstances when making decisions.

Max Gerber emigrated from Russia to the U.S. when he was seven years old. He was the fifth of eight children. He was an avid reader, self-educated, and valued education. He encouraged his children to seek the highest level possible. He was a devoted husband and father. As an entrepreneur, he built Gerber Plumbing Fixtures from the ground up. Harriet learned about business relationships, education, and management from her father through his example.

Harriet said her father was a fascinating man. He was her role model and her best friend. He treated employees with respect and made it a point to know all their names. Harriet admired her father's business philosophy. He would tell Harriet to remember to take one step at a time, that she could only eat one meal at a time or wear one dress at a time.

Harriet also learned about the importance of philanthropy from her father. Stirred by his influence, Harriet has donated considerable hours and dollars to a number of organizations including the Jewish United Fund, the U.S. Holocaust Memorial Museum, American Israel Chamber of Commerce and Industry, North Shore Auxiliary of the Jewish Children's Bureau, Mount Sinai Hospital Service Club, and Brandeis University. In recognition of her generosity, Harriet has received the Deborah Award and the Julius Rosenwald Award. She also is the only woman to be elected to the National Plumbing Hall of Fame.

Like Harriet, Ruby M. H. Frank, Founder and President of Frank's Employment, Inc., looked to her parents as role models. Ruby said they helped her elevate her standards and goals. Her parents sent all their children to college in the 1930s and 1940s when a college education wasn't appreciated by the general public. Ruby said her parents encouraged her and her siblings to "make something" of themselves.

Ruby's parents raised their children with a strong sense of civic duty and the value of hard work. They also taught Ruby about business in ways like trading housekeeping for piano lessons. Growing up in North Dakota, Ruby said her father was the only veterinarian in the area, and her mother was a marvelous homemaker. They always were very busy with work, church, and community activities.

Following in her parents' footsteps, Ruby has participated in numerous organizations and served on over a dozen boards including Delnor-Community Hospital, Baker Hotel Living Center, and The Aurora Foundation. She is listed in Who's Who in Finance and Industry, Who's Who in American Women, Who's Who In Midwest, and Who's Who in Executive and Professional Women. She also has received an impressive list of awards including The Charlemagne Award and Executive of the Year 1982.

Ruby created her temporary and permanent employment agency in 1957. Few women were working in the 1950s, much less creating their own business in addition to raising a family and actively participating in community responsibilities. Ruby modeled herself after her parents' examples of courage, strength, community responsibility, and in the importance of keeping busy.

Professional Examples

Superiors often teach us as much about how not to manage personnel or business as how to do it effectively. Adult Probation Supervisor Ingrid Sharos reminds us to examine the actions of our superiors and the results that follow their actions. We then can modify the examples of even the best superiors to fit our own style and situation. Ingrid said in her career she sees certain people who have very valuable insights and knowledge. But that doesn't necessarily mean she wants to be exactly like them.

Debra Trent is an artist and "No Limits for Women Artists" leader. "No Limits" workshops help women artists to define a vision of their future as an artist, the steps to achieve that vision, and the support they need to get there. Looking to role models helps Debra define her own goals and the path to attain those goals.

Debra said she is inspired by the works of poet Audrey Lorde and writer Bell Hooks. She also admires the women from the farming community in Wisconsin where she was raised. Some of those women no longer are alive, but Debra said she remembers them and the way they lived. She found those dynamic women to be amazing and fine examples for her to emulate.

Dr. Jeannette Martens Sorrentino's professional role model was her family dentist, Paul Krolik. She admired his rapport with patients and entered the dental field, at least in part, because of him. She even worked for him her first three years as a dentist. Now, as an independent contractor for Zachary Soiya, DDS, she continues to watch and learn. "I'm still evolving," said Jeannette. "I'm not there yet, wherever 'there' is."

Jeannette said she also learned from many of the nuns and female professors at the colleges she attended including Purdue and St. Mary's Notre Dame (for her BS), DePaul (for her Masters Degree), and Loyola (for her DDS). Jeannette said the women she admired most were energetic and "knew their stuff."

Leslie Wheeler Hortum is the Senior Vice President for Federation Development for the U.S. Chamber of Commerce. She is the first woman to be appointed that position in the Chamber's 85 year history. Leslie said her role model is Elizabeth Dole. She has examined Mrs. Dole's position with the American Red Cross and learned from her actions. Leslie said she was impressed with Mrs. Dole because she recognized the strength of volunteers and even volunteered to work her first year without pay. Leslie said she admires Elizabeth Dole's smarts and her compassion.

Chapter Five

FIRST IMPRESSIONS

One of my favorite patchwork quilt patterns is called log cabin. It's a popular pattern, one we have seen many times. Strips of fabric are sewn around a center square to form a block, and then these blocks are sewn together to form the quilt. The strips of fabric represent logs of a cabin. The center block is often red and represents the fire in the hearth.

The log cabin quilt is symbolic of the family. The ideal family is built on a solid and secure foundation. The center and heart of the family is love. I realize this representation isn't always the way it really is behind closed doors. Not every child is born into a loving, supportive family. We, who have been born with such a privilege, honor our parents for being our first mentors and giving us a positive start in life.

As parents we have the first opportunity and the first responsibility to mentor our children. We are the ones on which our children count to answer questions based on our own experience and knowledge or to link them with the resource or person that can help them. Through our words and actions we teach our children about life issues, values, unconditional and non-judgmental love, faith, and compassion. We also teach them about the mentoring relationship and the benefits of learning from people wiser and more experienced than ourselves.

Perhaps, when they become adults, we even can guide our children in their career. If we are in the same or similar profession, we can share our professional knowledge and experience, assist them with direction, and coach them on relations with peers, subordinates, and management. We might even be able to introduce our children to people we know who can offer them additional information or opportunity other than what we can offer.

Eye Physician and Surgeon Dr. Monique Anawis said she is very grateful for the mentoring that comes from her family. Her father, Dr. Emanuel Anawis, mother, Renee, and her grandmother have been her greatest source of support, encouragement, and guidance. Monique said her first mentors and her strongest ones still are her family.

Linaya Hahn, PMS educator and author, said her parents taught her about inner strength and self-esteem. They supported her even when they did not agree with her. They encouraged her sense of curiosity, which has been a driving force in her investigation into PMS. "My parents said I could do anything I wanted to do except cross the street alone when I was three years old," said Linaya.

Strong Mothers/Strong Daughters

Naming mothers as mentors was common among The Fabulous Fifty-Two. These successful women recognize the tremendous contribution their mothers made in their development and character. They talked of their mothers' strength and courage and how their mothers helped them become the successful women they are. American Medical Association President Dr. Nancy Wilson Dickey said she has learned so much from both of her parents, and particularly her mother. Nancy said had her mother been born in a different decade she would have gone way beyond Nancy's achievements.

The Fabulous Fifty-Two also appreciate their mother's honesty, even when it is hurtful to hear. They know their mothers have their best interest at heart. Director of WGN Television Traffic Jane Hayden said her mother, Bernadette Hayden, gives her good advice on life issues. Bernadette is strong and opinionated. Jane said her mother tells Jane when she's right or wrong because she loves her.

Diana Dionisio-Pieczynski is the manager of publicity and promotions at WGN-TV. Diana said her mother, Fran Dionisio, gave her excellent educational and career direction. "She helped me pick my major and school. She dragged my butt all around," Diana said.

Diana said her mother puts her daughter's best interests before her own when giving advice. When Diana had a job offer across the country, her mother told her to meet the challenge and take the opportunity. Fran realized Diana may never live close to her daughter again, but it was a good career move for Diana. Diana said she is grateful for her mother's ongoing common sense advice.

Ruth Martens, MD, D.Ht. is a medical doctor in general practice specializing in the use of classical homeopathy. Ruth said her mother, Lois Irene Martens, and grandmother, Lois Irene Williams, were the first people on which she relied. These women offered Ruth a childhood built on concrete advice, support, and laughter. Ruth said there was a wonderful balance between them building her confidence to do whatever she wanted to do and not making her feel as if she had to be a superwoman. Ruth added that she had tremendous respect for her grandmother. She said the woman was a pillar of strength under amazing odds.

My daughter, Erin, was around eleven years old when she wrote a poem which depicted our family as a puzzle and each one of us as a piece of that puzzle.

Erin wrote:

My mother is the four corners that holds our
family together.
My sister and I are the center pieces.
My brother is the piece that doesn't quite fit.
My father is the piece lost on the floor.

Erin saw what was happening in her family from a child's point of view, which may or may not be completely accurate, but was very sad. My only consolation was that she realized I was trying to hold the family together under trying times, and perhaps, she felt some comfort in that.

Leslie Wheeler Hortum, the Senior Vice President for Federation Development of the U. S. Chamber of Commerce, said her mother provided her and her brother with this type of stability in their home. Leslie was twelve years old when her father died. Leslie's mother, Louise Wheeler, went outside the home to work. She became the editor of the National Business Women's Magazine and was appointed a position in the Reagon/Bush Administration. As a single, working parent of two children, Louise maintained the financial and emotional well being of the family. Leslie said her mother made it all happen without making her or her brother feel they were neglected. Her mother pulled everything together and just kept right on going.

Of course, as our children become adults, their world may not be anything like ours. We may not understand or know how to develop our children's gifts, strengths, and needs. They may be in a profession of which we have little knowledge. They may have more education than we have. They may not even follow the same faith. But we can be available for support and mentoring in other areas possibly such as marriage, children, or values.

My mother, Patricia Doyle, was a wonderful home-maker. She was married to the same man, my father, for 49 years. My mother never worked outside of the home after my oldest brother was born. She devoted her life to cleaning, cooking, sewing, and caring for her five children and husband. She never learned how to drive a car or saw much of our country, much less of the world.

I am married for the third time, have three children and three stepchildren only ten to 14 years younger than I am. For many years, I either worked two jobs or worked one job and went to school in addition to caring for my children and home. Four years ago I married my husband, Marshall. The past few years I have had the privilege of being able to travel through the United States as well as Canada, Mexico, Latin America, and Europe.

My mother and I have lived very different life-styles, but much of the information she shared with me still applies. She taught me about cooking, housekeeping, and child-care. More importantly, she taught me about values, love, and how to make a house a home.

Dr. Amy Coene Bales said much the same thing about her mother, Beverly Coene. Beverly was a full-time at-home mom until Amy was about eight years old. As a cardiologist, Amy's life-style is very different than her mother's. Amy said her mother was always there. She was very patient, and put her kids first. Whenever Amy thinks of how she should be as a wife and mother, she thinks of her mother.

"I've chosen a different path than my mother," said Amy. "I can't be exactly like her, but I can try to put her example and advice to work for me in a different way. She helps me remember how important family is. My mother reminds me that twenty years from now my patients won't be at my side. Hopefully, my family will be," she said.

Five years ago Amy's focus was on her career and the competitive atmosphere of medicine. She is still devoted to her career and the investment she has in it, but she is aware of a personal transition in her priorities toward home and family. Amy said she started to change when she got married. She always thought she would work full time. Now she prefers to be home with her baby daughter. Amy said she struggles with 'mommy guilt' when she has to work a lot.

Bonds are strong enough between several of The Fabulous Fifty-Two and their mothers to outlive life itself. A number of these dynamic women still regard their mothers as mentors, even though they are no longer alive. The mother may be lost physically to the daughter, but that mother-daughter energy connection remains.

Actress Ann Jillian said her mother, Margaret, always has been, and always will be, her mentor. Margaret passed away in the spring of 1997. Ann continues to ask her mother for guidance. "She was my flagship through all phases of my life," said Ann. "She taught me to see God in every bit of creation. She taught me to stop and admire the rose, smell the flower, and remember He took time to make it for us."

Margaret also identified the talents in her daughter. She put Ann on stage at the age of four, took the family from Massachusetts to Hollywood, and invested large sums of money into dance and acting lessons for Ann. She was Ann's first manager. "My mother was one mover and shaker," said Ann.

Margaret knew when to charge ahead and when to step back. When Ann was ten-years old she starred as Little Bo Peep in the movie *Babes in Toyland*. Ann remembered her mother's response to Walt Disney when he wanted to change Ann's last name. Ann said in her mother's down-home good sense, she said to Mr. Disney, 'you know best' and stayed out of his way.

In 1985 Ann was diagnosed with cancer in both breasts. Margaret had breast cancer 20 years previously. So, although the situation was physically and emotionally challenging, Ann had learned how to get through it from her mother's example. Ann said her mother never stopped living. She squeezed every moment out of life.

Carole Miller is a Realtor and broker, President of the Women's Council of Realtors, and member of the Fox Valley Board of Realtors. Carole said to this day, even though her mother passed away in 1987, she calls on her mother for direction. She feels her mother hears her when she asks for help and responds to her call.

Carole said her mother mentored her in the art of understanding people and in common sense. Carole has so much respect for her mother today in retrospect. Her mother was a go-getter. She was inspiring and had an important impact on Carole. Her mother knew what Carole was thinking and what she needed before she knew, as if she could penetrate deep into her soul. Carole also said her mother was free with advice, even if she didn't ask for any.

As a musical contractor, booking agent, and president of Anita Smith Associates, Anita Smith links musicians with musicals such as *Phantom of the Opera, Les Miserables, Miss Saigon,* and *Joseph.* She is highly respected and successful in the industry. Anita's mother, Hilda, died five years ago from pancreatic cancer. Anita said no matter how old she is or how busy she is with her work, she continues to miss her mother's presence.

She said her mother was independent, ageless, and understanding. She was wise, honest, optimistic, and fair. "My mother, Hilda, was the epitome of what a mother should be," said Anita. "I could always count on her for good, solid advice, and I still do. When I ask her for help, I feel I get answers. If everybody could have a Hilda, their life would be so much better."

The Father Mentor

Fathers are no less important as mentors than mothers. They have their own gifts and viewpoints to offer. My father, John Doyle, is very open-minded. He listens without judging or telling me what to do. He has taught me how to think for myself, make my own decisions, and take responsibility for my words and actions. I am so grateful my father had me practice these vital skills in small doses as a child. When I was forced to make major life-changing choices, I was at least marginally experienced in decision-making.

Pamela Sullivan, Senior Vice President of TRW, Inc., said it is the level of self-esteem her father, Francis R. Sullivan, instilled in her for which she is most grateful. Her father believed she could and would be anything she wanted to be. He didn't think of her goals or education any differently than he did for her brothers. Pamela said her father wanted her to get her Ph.D. At 53 years old, Pamela said she doesn't think that many other women her age had fathers who thought that way.

Susan Schreter, the President and Cofounder of Caring Products International, a company which specializes in incontinence products, said her father, Robert Schreter, significantly influenced her business approach. Susan's father had several manufacturing companies when she was a child. He openly shared all aspects of the business world with his young daughter.

Robert would take her to the plants on weekends and allow her to sit in on meetings with advertisers, accountants, and attorneys. He created an interest for her in his business and its operations. He would present information such as why the plant was designed as it was, what concerned him in regards to labor, and why products were manufactured in a particular way. He would explain how his attendance at a convention related to the well-being of the family.

Susan said her father did not come from a privileged background. He, like her mother, worked hard and received their higher education by attending night school. Susan said her father taught her about stamina and courage in business and how one false move results in corporate death. He encourages her to pursue her ideas, investigate them, prepare herself personally and professionally, and act on her ideas once she knows what she is doing.

Extended Family Mentors

As I said earlier, I have a very large family. My mother's side, the McCarthy's, are numerous. They are practical and grounded. They are an interactive group. They enjoy getting together socially. Many work together in a family business. My father's side, the Doyle's, are considerably fewer in numbers. They are creative and technically adept. I don't see them as often as the McCarthys, but any one of them would help me if I asked.

Both sides have so much to offer. Someone is always available to go to for advice or support on just about any topic. Uncle Don Ripoli has helped me with my taxes, Uncle Tom McCarthy helped me write my first commercials, Aunt Paula McCarthy taught me about makeup when I was a teenager, and Aunt Marlene Ripoli supplied a strong shoulder and direction several times in my life when I experienced growing pains.

I am very fortunate to have such an extensive mentoring network. From grandmothers, when they were alive, down to cousins, I have had an assortment of resources at my fingertips. The variety complements what my parents alone can offer me.

Few people have such a diverse group of relatives to access for mentoring. Psychologist Dr. Sue (Susan) Holstein's family is quite small, but she does have a jewel in her aunt, Connie Delsolar. Sue said Aunt Connie taught her about family values and how to nurture relationships. She is available to Sue anytime, with open arms, a compassionate ear, and a full refrigerator.

Kathleen S. Freeland is a horticulturist, lecturer, and manager of marketing for Midwest Groundcovers. She said the most influential person in her private life was her grandmother. Her grandmother was strong and independent. She taught Kathleen the importance of taking care of and respecting herself.

Mentoring the Mentor

Mentoring is a reciprocal relationship. Teachers learn from students as well as the other way around. Sometimes even a very young child can be more insightful than an adult. Adults complicate situations with details, past negative experiences, and self-doubt. Children see the obvious. They look at things more simply and often more clearly than we can.

One time when Erin was about three years old, I was pouring shampoo from one bottle to another because I liked the squirt cap on the old bottle. Erin asked why I didn't just switch the caps. I knew from past experience that caps don't fit from bottle to bottle. I demonstrated this to Erin only to find the cap did fit. All I had to do was switch the caps.

We have the opportunity to learn from our children's experiences. As our children grow up, they choose different paths than our own, or ones that were not available to us years ago. My children are encountering so many different situations than I have and live under different circumstances than I did at their age.

Lisa is 23 years old. She has lived in Florida and Virginia in addition to our home state of Illinois. She is currently a marketing representative for a company that provides emergency helicopter and ambulance transportation. At 20 years of age, Erin is attending Marquette University in Wisconsin and majoring in nursing. Joey is barely an adult at 18 years of age. He is an athlete and an artist. Being a teenaged male, his perspective is not like mine or his sisters. Looking at the world through my children's eyes encourages me to see ideas and viewpoints that I would not have seen without them.

Linaya Hahn said, in addition to her parents, her two sons, Christopher and Gregory Back, also have mentored her. She said they assisted her personal growth emotionally, spiritually, and practically when she began her research into PMS.

Carol Havey has many talents. She is a retired nurse, author of *Women and Self-Confidence: How to Take Charge of Your Life*, public speaker, dancer, artist, fashion designer, volunteer, and mother of seven children. She said in addition to her 100 year-old mother, who is her long-term mentor, she also learns from her grown children and children-in-law. Their expertise lies in a wide assortment of areas including computers, medicine, accounting, business, and management. Carol taps into all of her children's and children-in-law's current and extensive skills and knowledge. She said this approach is sensible, practical, and necessary, because they take her into the future. "If you are not going ahead these days, you are falling behind," said Carol.

Chapter Six

TEACHERS ARE LEADERS

There is more to education than what goes on in the classroom. That's what my daughter, Lisa, told me when she was accepted at Northwood University in Florida. She said the experience of going across the country for her last two years of college would be vital to her education in life as well as her business major. She would discover her strengths and weaknesses by living on her own. The experience would develop her decision-making capabilities. She said her grades would improve. Being so far from friends and activities at home, she would be less distracted from her studies.

Now I know she was conning me with her method of persuasion. Lisa was thinking about the Northwood University brochure that pictured cute guys studying on the beach. She envisioned herself next to those young men. She would be suntanned and her long hair would blow in the breeze while she sipped something stronger than iced tea. Text books would be buried somewhere in the sand next to her beach towel.

I also knew there was truth in her statement. There is more to education than what is taught in the classroom. The list of educational opportunities is endless in this very interconnected world of ours. We have much to learn from hands-on experiences with technology, travel destinations, and especially people of differing backgrounds, abilities, and talents.

We learn segments of information from everyone around us. We ask a store technician how to connect our new VCR to our television. A neighbor shows us how to change a flat tire on our car. Our sister teaches us yoga. Hair stylists teach us how to care for our hair. Counselors teach us how to cope and overcome.

However, the classroom is an environment designed specifically to promote learning, and teachers are in strategic positions to extend the educational experience beyond the syllabus, to be more than dispensers of information. Day after day, for the length of the course, or possibly the entire school year, teachers have captive audiences of students. They have unlimited opportunity to become leaders of the classroom community. Teachers who mentor can motivate students to think for themselves, discover the joy of learning, find ways of applying text book information, look to new directions, and develop personally, psychologically, spiritually, physically, and intellectually.

Recently my son, Joey, and I had a discussion about our favorite teachers. In his 15 years of school counting two years of preschool, kindergarten, five years of elementary school, three years of middle school, and nearly four years of high school, he has had about 75 teachers. This includes general education as well as elective classes such as art, physical education, home economics, music, and catechism. He also has had about twenty-five coaches for baseball, football, and basketball. Out of all those teachers and coaches, Joey remembers about eight to be outstanding in additon to a very powerful high school counselor and mentor, Linda McCulloch. He said he grew personally as well as intellectually from these nine educators. That number of wonderful teachers, coaches, and counselors also means that the other 91, for any number of reasons, were no more to him than ones who inform.

Teachers Who Mentor
Produce Teachers Who Mentor

I've had a lot more teachers than Joey, but even I only can come up with a handful that were more than an instructor. Those few were extraordinary. Biology Professor Barbara Anderson from College of DuPage revealed the magnificence of a world in which I had not appreciated before taking her classes. I've never seen another teacher work as hard as Barbara at presenting material in a dynamic and memorable way.

Pat Puccio is another fine example of a mentoring teacher. Pat was my psychology professor at College of DuPage. I was struggling personally when I attended her class. She invited me to meet with her for ten minutes each morning to discuss some of the challenges I was facing. I learned about psychology from her in the classroom. I also learned about my own psyche and grew considerably because of our morning sessions. Pat reached out to me on a personal level and helped me ease through a transitional part of my life. She taught me how to recognize my needs and discover ways to meet those needs.

The educators of The Fabulous Fifty-Two expressed this same desire to be teachers who mentor. Several years ago Carole Miller was a principal at a correctional facility governed by the Department of Corrections. The position was more than an administrative job to Carole. It was a chance to promote education and be a positive catalyst in young troubled lives. Carole said nothing makes her happier than to have one of her previous students tell her they graduated high school and are attending classes at a university.

PMS educator Linaya Hahn also expects mentoring to be a part of her teaching. The central message she delivers is that PMS is real and that women don't have to have it. But merely passing on that message is not enough. She also is a resource for extensive research findings on causes and alternative options in dealing with PMS. Linaya said she does not impose her direction on clients, but when they ask for suggestions, she shows them how to get out of their own way.

Barbara Junceau is a teacher/mentor who was mentored by several teachers and educational advisors. When teaching astrology, she encourages questions and comments. She expects to be approached by students after presenting class material. She is available to answer questions or to point students in directions where they can receive answers. And when astrological questions touch personal, emotional, psychological, or spiritual nerves, Barbara supports individualized growth of students on all these levels.

She said this approach is important to her because of the mentors she had in her education. Barbara said she took a great deal from them and integrated their teachings into her work. She was privileged to have had people in her life who took time to talk and work with her.

Barbara's high school guidance counselor, Dorothy Allen, guided her personal development as a leader. Barbara excelled in academics. She was in sports and the editor of the yearbook. She said Mrs. Allen was always on her case. She pushed her well past where Barbara wanted to go.

Another mentor was the Professor of Religion and Baptist minister, Jane Bennet. Barbara was Jane's assistant for all four years in school. Jane was supportive when Barbara's brother died. She trusted Barbara to grade papers and work closely with her. But Barbara said the relationship was also a bit adversarial. They didn't think in the same terms. In fact they rarely agreed. Barbara often challenged Jane's ideas with her words and papers. Barbara said she respected and loved Jane dearly, even though they thought differently. Through that experience, she learned two people didn't have to share the same thoughts to love each other and work side-by-side.

Another significant mentor in Barbara's life was the president of the college, Dr. William Litterick. He spent hour after hour talking to her in his office. "In his own way he let me know early on who I was and that he was there for me as a consultant and supporter. He validated my thoughts and potential for success," Barbara said.

One time Barbara got into serious trouble with faculty members for bucking the status quo. Doctor Litterick approached Barbara and said he respected her for taking a stand. Barbara never expected the president to react in that manner. She said that is when the real mentoring began. Doctor Litterick never criticized her, but he pushed her thinking beyond where she was.

Barbara's most influential mentor was Dorthea Spellman, a faculty member of the school of social work at the University of Denver. Women were a minority in campus ministry at that time. Barbara said male colleagues often found it awkward with Barbara on the staff. Barbara was the only female member of the YMCA-YWCA Board of Directors in the campus ministry at the university, so she looked to Dorthea for guidance. Barbara respected and admired Dorthea. She said she "bounced her thoughts" off of her and trusted Dorthea's judgment and friendship.

Dorthea helped Barbara apply spiritual ethics in an administration of both the student YMCA-YWCA and the office of chaplains. She also helped Barbara learn how to deal with spirituality and political issues of the university and the world outside its doors. Dorthea died many years ago, but Barbara said Dorthea continues to live on in her heart and head.

"She helped me become self-confident, self-aware, and mature personally and professionally, which is no small thing to accomplish," said Barbara. "One of Dorthea's truths that still echoes in me is that leaders are the least free people of all. By her belief in me as a professional, I learned to believe in myself and the responsibilities I have as a leader."

Archeologist Dr. Diana Craig Patch also acknowledged the teachers/mentors who impacted her teaching. Diana has a Ph.D. in Egyptology. She was appointed adjunct assistant professor, lecturer, and graduate teaching associate at several universities and colleges. She credits Marilyn Waldman, Professor of Islamic History at Ohio State University where Diana received her Ph.D. in anthropology, for significantly influencing her own approach to teaching, an approach that gives students direction in addition to information. Diana said Professor Waldman was the finest teacher she ever met. Diana could never imitate the Professor successfully, but she keeps her style in mind.

Diana's first giant leap into the field occurred in the summer of 1971, just before her senior year of high school, when she received a scholarship to the Field Museum of Natural History's anthropology program. The following summer she attended an archeology program sponsored at Northwestern University. There, she met two women bioanthropologists who were demanding and indifferent to her, although they taught her about archeology and the ability of women to pursue careers in the field.

But it was Archeology Professor Patty Jo Watson at Washington University who was the first person to be more than an educator to Diana. Patty Jo was Diana's advisor. She took Diana into the field in Kentucky to assist her as a freshwater molluscan fauna specialist for the work on her archeological shell mounds. She helped Diana get a position on a French dig in Susa, Iran. Patty Jo and her husband, Red Watson, also helped Diana recover from a terrible car accident.

Diana said Patty Jo changed her life. She is brilliant, kind, and supportive. She taught Diana how to be a scholar. Diana said Pat and Red are truly the most incredible people she has ever met. Not only for what they taught her about archeology, others could have taught that, although without as much insight, but about people and life.

Diana was fortunate to have another mentor, Professor David O'Connor from the University of Pennsylvania where she received her Ph.D. in Egyptology. Professor O'Connor helped her make the actual move into Egyptology as a career by trusting her to run an entire archeology expedition to Egypt without a supervisor. That was the first time a woman held such a responsibility in Egyptology.

Guided Imagery and Music (GIM) founder, violinist, and violin teacher, Dr. Helen Bonny, said her music professors were always more than just teachers to her. Her first music instructor, Karl Kuersteiner, taught her piano from the age of nine through high school. Helen said Mr. Kuersteiner was a gentle person and offered just what she needed.

Reber Johnson, Helen's violin teacher at Oberlin Conservatory of Music, was similar in his approach. Helen said the teacher was a tough task master but appreciative of her as a person.

Helen went into music therapy when she was 40 years

old. She took her music in that direction after an enlightening experience at an epiphany service. She wanted to offer other people the opportunity to have a spiritual encounter, also. Her professor at the time understood Helen's motives but advised her to keep her mysticism to herself. Helen said he never changed his mind about that, but became a very significant friend and mentor. He was supportive of her work and kept her grounded.

Allison Barnett is a writer, graphic artist, and illustrator for Moonwolf Graphics+ and also is a T'ai Chi Ch'uan instructor for Barnett Martial Arts. She said she strives to be a teacher who mentors, because her teacher/mentors helped her focus her direction in art and writing into a profession she loves. Allison has been writing stories and drawing since she was a child. In high school, she was awarded a scholarship for classes at Art Center College of Design in Pasadena, California. She said what she learned from her art teacher there was invaluable to her career.

She also named several college professors at California State University-San Bernadino as being influential. B.H. (Pete) Fairchild, a creative writing professor, showed her how to communicate in a way she had never known before. He identified her talent with words as well as her varied interests in the arts. He encouraged her to become more than just a better writer. Allison said Professor Fairchild was interested in her as a whole person, and he was very sensitive to what she could bring to her poetry.

Recognizing Teachers Who Make the Mark

Often what appears to us as two unrelated events or situations in our lives are later recognized to be substantially interconnected. Eye surgeon Dr. Monique Anawis was introduced to ice skating at a Brownie Girl Scout out-ing. She loved the experience and wanted to take lessons so she could learn to skate backwards. The lessons she took from Coach Debbie Storey taught her life skills as well as how to skate. Monique said she never could have imagined the impact that one moment of wanting to skate backwards would have on her life.

Monique skated and entered competitions from age eight to about eighteen. When she reached the end of her high school years, Monique had to decide whether to pursue a path to the Olympics or continue her education to college. Her decision was education, but the skills and techniques she learned have been lifelong, enhancing not only her young skating career but also her medical career. Monique said Debbie was concerned with her skating as an adjunct to her academic and life goals. She was devoted to her and helped formulate her attitude about life in general. Monique feels fortunate to have had Debbie as her coach.

From Debbie, Monique learned to carry a notebook and write down daily strengths and weakness and how weaknesses can become strengths. She learned visualization — how to rehearse an athletic performance in her mind previous to an event. She learned the importance of thorough preparation, not only being prepared to perform a routine with optimum ability but also to consider above and beyond the necessary supplies, such as extra musical tapes and costumes.

She discovered the importance of maintaining a positive attitude. A shy child, Monique learned to maintain composure and self-confidence before large audiences. She learned how to travel to events easily and efficiently and appreciate travel as an opportunity to learn from new places and people.

Monique said she uses the notebook, careful preparation, positive thinking, and visualization to this day in her practice. These techniques are tremendously helpful, because, when the time comes to do surgery, she feels like she has been there before.

Physician and Classical Homeopathic Specialist Dr. Ruth Martens said she positively was influenced by many teachers in her academic years. Ruth was a gifted child. Math and science were her favorite classes. She also had an interest in music, playing piano, French horn, and cello. Ruth said she needed more from instructors than excellent teaching ability because class work was not typically challenging for her. Ruth aligned herself with teachers who personalized studies to meet her intellectual capacity and taught her to think for herself. Ruth said she remembers the ones who gave her something more. She remembers the ones who challenged her.

Ruth was tall for her age and wore glasses and braces. She identified with two female teachers who also were tall. She said she learned from them how to walk down the street and not be ashamed of being tall or smart or anything else.

Dentist Dr. Jeannette Martens Sorrentino said she didn't interact with other children or do typical "kids stuff" when she was a child. She said she was surrounded by adults. Her parents were German-born, quiet and hard working. When Jeannette was seven years old, she became very sick. She was diagnosed with a brain tumor, which was successfully removed. The following year she had surgery on her eye.

Her childhood life-style, illnesses, and recovery resulted in Jeannette's desire to use her life in a personally meaningful way. Jeannette's parents supported her dreams and encouraged her to pursue higher education. She considered law, medicine, and finally, dentistry. While in graduate school she worked in the lab under Dr. Robert Thommes. Jeannette said Dr. Thommes taught and mentored her. He expanded her interests in science and the goal of entering the field as a profession.

When Geochemist Marcia E. Balestri was a child, she liked examining and learning about rocks. She took classes in chemistry and geology in high school and college. She names her high school chemistry teacher, Mr. Gaskins, as one of her first mentors in the field of science. Marcia said Mr. Gaskins was so enthusiastic about teaching he prompted her to want to know more. She even stayed after school to work in his lab.

Then in graduate school, her advisor, Dr. Brookins, directed her scientific interests toward a career. Marcia said he gave her great advice without standing over her shoulder. He turned her loose with gentle guidance.

Educational Groups Rooted in Mentoring

Looking back to chapter three of this book, several of the educational programs that were highlighted deliberately integrate mentoring into the learning process. Kathy Ballman's degree program at Prescott College in Arizona and the GIM program at the Bonny Foundation are based on learning through mentors. These types of educational programs recognize the interaction between a teacher and student to be vital. The presentation of necessary material is only a portion of the learning process. The human element of a mentor allows for customized development. Through mentoring, protégés have access to their own personal ally who supports and feeds their growth.

East Coast Psychotherapist Alice Umbach enrolled in such a program that she said changed her life. Alice had three young children in the 1960s when she longed to go back to school. Students over 30 years of age were not welcome at colleges during that time. Nor was it socially acceptable for a wife and mother to take educational classes. Women were to send their children off to school in the morning, pick them up at school midday for lunch, and be home for them when school let out in the afternoon.

When a woman worked or attended school, it signified her disregard for her children's welfare and a husband's inadequacy to financially support his family. Alice said that one of the worst things that could happen would be for school to call home because a child was sick, and the mother was at a class or working. It was more acceptable for her to be on the tennis courts.

Alice found the transition to college easier after enrolling in noncredit classes at Greener Fields, a nonprofit three-room school for women. Greener Fields offered classes in psychology, philosophy, and history in a safe, non-judgmental, nonthreatening environment. Alice said Greener Fields was a fabulous place to help women expand their minds and horizons. The instructors promoted the idea of education for the sake of learning. They sent her in a direction she wouldn't have gone without them by giving her the courage and support to go for a degree.

Caring Products International's President Susan Schreter said the college she attended, Smith College in Western Massachusetts, was a source of guidance and support. The Ivy League school was founded by Sofia Smith over a hundred years ago. The focus at Smith is on women and their development. Course work includes the contributions of women in each study, such as the contribution of women in medieval history or World War II. Students are encouraged to investigate, question, and formulate ideas. They are given opportunities to grow and succeed.

Students are recognized for their great potential to succeed by every member of the administration, staff, and alumni. Susan said she is very grateful to have attended the college. The Smith philosophy helped define the person she is today.

Music therapist, performer, producer, and song writer Louise Dimiceli-Mitran found a catalyst for personal growth in weekend seminars of The Women Within. The Women Within directs women on a journey into their inner self. The program is about women empowering women.

Female facilitators lead small and large group sessions in meditation. They help students penetrate personal blocks and reconnect with feminist values. They teach how to listen without being judgmental and how to tap into their inner strengths. All social expectations are left outside the center. Students wear no makeup, jewelry, or nail polish. Louise said participants end up reclaiming parts of their self that was lost for whatever reason. She claimed the women at The Women Within changed her life.

The young need old men. They need
men who are not ashamed of age, not
pathetic imitations of themselves. . . .
Parents are the bones on which children sharpen their teeth.

Peter Ustinov
Dear Me (1977), ch 18.

Chapter Seven

PEER MENTORSHIP

Rebecca Nyce sat next to me during classes at Judson College every week for a year and a half. We shared class notes, resources, and snacks. She helped me through my mother's illness. I helped her through a divorce. Being nearly twenty years apart in age, we offered one another perspectives from two different generations.

I haven't talked to Rebecca in quite a while, but that doesn't lessen the kindness and assistance we shared. Nor does it mean that we no longer care about each other's happiness. It is just that circumstances have taken us down different roads that rarely connect anymore.

Most friendships are really peer mentorships. They are as varied as the ways we meet and the situations we encounter. These relationships tend to come and go with job, neighborhood, religious, social, club, and activity changes. We can be very close to these people for a period of time and then lose contact as we move along our way.

We align ourselves with people who relate to our current situation and can give us answers, personal examples of their experiences, and support. We are drawn to people who we feel can understand us, our feelings and our needs, and who can share answers they know about this complicated world in which we live.

Music therapist Louise Dimiceli-Mitran had one peer mentor who came to her out of a situation that was otherwise discouraging. Louise's voice teacher at Drake University told her she cold not sing, that she had no talent. Art Department Secretary Marilyn Condon disagreed. She rallied to Louise's side, supplying her with the encouragement and direction she did not get from the voice teacher. Louise said she doesn't know if she would have gotten through college without Marilyn and may not have become a professional singer, musician, and music therapist if she had not come forward.

Louise also aligned herself with Soozie Cotter-Schaeufele. Soozie was the first woman Louise could relate to on a professional level. Louise had some male musical mentors along the way, but she said the men did not see the whole picture for which she was striving. Soozie had the same approach as Louise had. A level of trust and sistership existed between them.

Our professional or personal situation does not have to be identical with someone else's for us to value their wisdom as a peer mentor. When the values, ethics, and purpose are similar or respected between two people, concrete guidance can be shared. Independent Registered Nurse Debbie (Debra) McElroy, RN, BSN, MPH said Ingrid Sharos, Supervisor for Adult Probations, is her friend and peer mentor. Debbie said they have very different job titles but similar responsibilities at work and in their private lives.

Work procedures and projects, relationships, children, school board matters, and family illness are topics on which they discuss and share solutions based on experiences. Debbie said Ingrid is a wonderful sounding board. She challenges her personally and professionally. Debbie respects what Ingrid thinks and how she thinks.

Mentoring may be one-way or mutual. Most of my friendships are very interactive with randomly balanced doses of giving and taking. A few have the scale tipped in a direction of me needing them more than they need me or the other way around. I have had a couple of friends who called constantly when they were in crisis and then faded out of my life. I also have had friends who allowed me to lean on them in times of my own crisis and then cut me from their lives when I could stand on my own, as if they only needed my neediness.

Peer mentors come about in a variety of ways. Some of my most valuable peer mentors were introduced to me by someone else. I have friends such as Mike and Marijo Pope who have been long-time friends of my husband, and Linda Lewis and Kim Przybyl who are my son Joey's friends' mothers. I probably would not have met these people without that personal link between us.

Social clubs, schools, and sports teams offer the opportunity to belong to groups of friends. Like a family, these groups have an overall personality. They have the ability to mentor as a whole and as individual components.

Mary Ellen Cory Collins, Sue Creedon Kezios, and Sally Berliner Thomas are friends I met while in high school. Each of us has grown and changed over nearly a thirty-year period, but the bond that we formed at the age of sixteen remains intact. Our relationship was, and remains to be, both a set of wings and a safety net. Individually and as a group, we have helped, and occasionally even pushed, each other to heights we dared to reach. We also have picked up the pieces after one of us have fallen. We have supported and offered guidance to each other through dating, marriages, miscarriages, job changes, divorces, illnesses, the trials and tribulations of children, and the deaths of extended family members. Months pass without us talking or getting together, and yet we know that all we have to do is pick up the phone, and a loving ear will be on the other end.

Louise Dimiceli-Mitran also has a group of peer mentors. She became friends with Theresa McNally, Mary Kay Tobin, and Jann Borta in high school and college. Their long history has endured school, job changes, marriages, and moving in different directions of the country. The group corresponds regularly over the telephone and meet one weekend a year for catch-up time and personal and group development.

All four women are in the healing arts and have holistic viewpoints on client approach. They have many similarities in their family situations. Their children are close in age and husbands like each other. They have supported each other financially and emotionally. They spur each other intellectually. Louise said she feels very lucky to have such a group of friends.

Ruth A. Chodak, Vice President of Business Development for the University of Chicago Hospitals and Health System, has a relationship with a group of women that spans three generations. Ruth is in her 40s, Jackie is in her 60s, and Hazel is in her 80s. Once a month the three women meet for dinner and conversation.

Ruth, Jackie, and Hazel became acquainted four years ago at Weiss Memorial Hospital where Ruth works. They started meeting after Hazel's husband died. Hazel was devastated after her husband's death. Ruth and Jackie offered her compassion and friendship.

Both Hazel and Ruth were married to surgeons and could identify with each other's marital situation. Ruth said all three women share a special relationship. They take care of each other. They've experienced similar problems but have different viewpoints. Ruth said Hazel and Jackie are very special ladies. She looks up to the older women with respect and feels a connection to them.

No Limits for Women Artists is a nationwide program structured to network artists to a group of peers in the arts, offsetting the isolation they typically experience. Fine artists, graphic artists, sculptors, poets, storytellers, musicians, dancers, and writers are invited to attend No Limits workshops. Many become friends and long-time peer mentors after the workshop's completion.

Participants are asked to answer aloud to the questions "What is your vision? What steps must you take to achieve it? What stands in your way? and What type of support do you need?" Fellow artists are required to listen to answers without verbally or physically responding. Not even a nod of the head is allowed until the speaker requests their support and direction. For many, it is the first time participants are able to voice thoughts and ideas uninterrupted.

No Limits workshop national leader and sculptor Debra Trent said, "if every single woman, man, and child was listened to, we would all know our hearts desire. We would have a vision and know the steps we must take to achieve it."

No Limits was developed by New York performing artist Betsy Damon who believed that women are socialized to set limits to their success. She also believed women were not represented fairly in the arts. A recent mailing by the National Museum of Women in the Arts reinstated that belief. The letter noted that the current edition of Janson's History of Art, one of the most widely distributed art history textbooks on college campuses, listed 575 artists, of whom 38 were women. The National Endowment for the Arts' 1990 statistics showed that 52.5% of all painters, sculptors, craft artists, and art print makers were women. Therefore less than 7% of the women artists were represented in the textbook.

Debra said the mentoring which occurs as a result of the No Limits workshops is valuable to the participant's continued progress. The shared mentoring builds relationships with other artists thereby encouraging each other's success and opportunities for representation. The women help enrich each other and grow in direction. They learn to recognize their needs and wants. They set goals together and point out possibilities they might not otherwise have seen.

Fruits of Our Labors

Many of the friends I have today I met through my work. In the process of writing profiles for newspapers, I would get to know the subjects personally. Angelic Facilitator Rev. M. Sue Storm, T'ai Chi Ch'uan instructor Herb Barnett, Comedian-Magician Ken Mate, even my husband, Marshall, were once subjects of feature stories I wrote for the *Chicago Tribune*. Writing about them exposed me to their personalities from the inside out. Once our friendships were established, little was left to be misinterpreted or misunderstood. I know who they are, where they've been, what they've done, and why. I know the rough road they've tread and the pain they have endured, and therefore I know how to tiptoe around the tender spots. I also know their private triumphs in addition to their public accomplishments.

Few people are privy to the depth of personal history and character of their friends as I just described. However, most work environments set a stage to become acquainted with co-workers and build friendships purely because they spend time together on a daily basis. Attorney Vicky Bush-Joseph met two of her closest friends and peer mentors through her work. After the death of her baby, Vicky said she made a decision to use her professional expertise in a positive, uplifting way. Attorneys Shelley Bostick and Terri Horwich helped Vicky see that decision become reality.

Shelley approached Vicky and Terri about joining forces to establish the law firm, Bostick, Bush-Joseph & Horwich. The plan was to limit the firm to helping intended parents with collaborative contracts such as surrogacies and adoptions. The unusual practice gave Vicky an opportunity to make the professional change she was seeking. Vicky said both Terri and Shelley, who recently moved out of state and left the firm, are her peer mentors. Vicky said she and Terri wouldn't have come as far as they have if Shelley hadn't taken them under her wing and taught them as much as she did. The women care about their clients and feel good about the work they do.

Archeologist Dr. Diana Craig Patch said Sharon Fetter is one of her best friends, strongest supporters, and advisors. Sharon was Diana's assistant director for several months on a field collection in the Egyptian low desert in 1982. Sharon read Diana's drafts of articles and provided constructive criticism. She has continued to be a friend and mentor. Sharon has always been available to advise Diana as to what research will or will not work out. Diana said Sharon encourages her when she is ready to quit.

Ingrid Sharos said supervisors are responsible for the professional development of employees, and therefore, she views all her supervisors as mentors. Ingrid said we must be able to approach our supervisor, or one from another department, for ideas, different perspectives, and help in keeping balanced.

In addition to supervisors, Ingrid has developed a profound relationship with one of her peers. She job-shares her position as an adult probations supervisor. Her partner works Monday and Tuesday, they both work Wednesday, and Ingrid works Thursday and Friday of each week. Ingrid said such sharing of professional space also promotes a high level of personal interaction. They know each other well enough to point out their shortcomings and pull each other in a better direction.

Sibling Reveling

I was born grown up. I liked mothering my younger brother and sisters and even my older brother. My sister Patti is exactly two years younger than I am. We share the same birthday - May 31. From a very young age, I liked to pretend I was her mother. The drawback to acting like an adult when I was a child was that I was then evaluated as a parent-figure.

Patti and I had a conversation sometime after we had both graduated from high school. She told me how she resented some of the things I had done to her when she was a child. She was upset about how I dressed her in mismatched clothes when she was four, how I made her mushy cereal for breakfast when she was six, and how when we played house I always had to be the mother. I apologized for hurting her and reminded her that, I too was a child at the time. I was six to eight years old when these things happened. After saying this to Patti, a spark of revelation crossed her face. She had never thought of me as a child, especially at that time.

Sibling rivalry is typical in most families. Sibling admiration also is common. Little brothers and sisters look up to older brothers and sisters. The little ones watch and trust the path the older one is treading to be the correct one to follow. When Eta-Lyn Lampert, Executive Assistant to Master Magician Lance Burton, was a child, she looked up to her big sister. Eta-Lyn saw in her sister what she did not see in herself. She thought her sister was smart, pretty, and had many friends. She desperately wanted to be like her sister. Eta-Lyn has only recently come to recognize the beauty she has within herself and the ability she has to choose her own path.

As my siblings and I have grown into adults, we have developed a level of respect for each of our individual strengths, experience, and wisdom. We tap into each other's gifts and assist each other in our own personal growth.

My brothers, sisters, and brother-in-laws form a unique entity. My older brother Mike (John Michael) knows about cars and telephones. My younger brother Jimmy is an expert in sound systems and biking. He also is a wonderful single parent. My brother-in-laws, Parke and Jimmy, are skilled craftsmen and are always ready to offer a helping hand.

My sister Patti is an expert financial planner, avid gardener, and can swing a hammer with the best of them. My other sister, Margaret, is the family organizer and planner. She is a keen sale and comparison shopper. I am creative. In addition to writing, I enjoy sewing and decorating. I also study alternative health and practice T'ai Chi Ch'uan and Chi Kung.

Between us, we have a wide range of resources. In addition to our basic skills, we look to each other for guidelines on wisdom, values, ethics, and intuition. When one of us has a need or question that another can help us with, we go to that sibling for guidance.

A number of The Fabulous Fifty-Two said they, too, revel in their relationship with siblings and share wisdom. Sisters particularly have formed dynamic bonds. Author and public speaker on women and self-confidence, Carol Havey said her older sister always has helped her see the road ahead. Two years older, Carol's sister typically experiences situations just before Carol. The sisters share their experiences and what does and does not work for them.

Siblings in similar life situations rely on each other for day-to-day guidance. Diana Dionisio-Pieczynski, WGN-TV Manager of Publicity and Promotions, said her sisters are mentors. Diana has one young son. Both of her sisters are married and have children. Diana and her sisters compare notes on their experiences and the results of their methods, especially in regards to parenting.

Significant Others Make Significant Mentors

Dr. Cheryl Conover, Professor of Medicine at the Mayo Clinic, said that when mentoring exists in both your personal and professional life, you have the opportunity to grow completely. Each part of your life enhances the other. Cheryl said the two most important factors for success are having mentors in your profession and marrying the right person. Her husband, Jack Thomas, is a skilled educator and public speaker. Cheryl and her husband support and assist each other where needed, which has been vital to their overall growth and success.

Many of The Fabulous Fifty-Two recognized their husbands' contribution to their personal and/or professional development. Pamela Sullivan, the senior vice-president of TRW, Inc., said her husband is by far the most skilled person she knows in business. She considers him a valuable mentor. Pamela said her husband is "an infinite influence in her life."

Licensed Clinical Psychologist Dr. Sue Holstein said her life has been enriched greatly by her husband, Attorney

Mark Holstein. She admires his positive attitude. Sue and Mark also learn about the human psyche and how to improve their communication skills with people in crisis by sharing experiences from their practices. Sue said Mark is an excellent problem solver. He has the ability to identify a problem and generate achievable solutions. He cuts through the fluff and recognizes the bottom line.

Both Carol Havey and Louise Dimiceli-Mitran said their husbands are their best friends and mentors. Carol said her husband has more integrity than anyone she has ever met.

Louise and her husband, Andy Mitran, write and produce music for their company, Mitran Mitran Music. They also conduct drumming seminars. "I love Andy's talent. He is gifted in different things than I am," said Louise. "We understand each others' music."

Diana Dionisio-Pieczynski said she and her husband, Richard Pieczynski, mentor each other, using one another as sounding boards. She said they bounce things off of each other quite frequently.

Allison Barnett, graphic artist and T'ai Chi Ch'uan instructor, said her husband, Herb Barnett, more than fed her personal growth. He turned her life around. According to Allison, when she met Herb she was functioning in disaster mode. She was physically and emotionally unhealthy and wondering why she couldn't get any part of her life to work. Herb helped Allison become a stronger, more secure person. He taught her how to live in the moment and remain grounded. He showed her how to stand on her own two feet, see herself for whom she is, and move forward in a positive direction. Allison said she would not have gotten where she is today without Herb.

"Opposites attract" is a saying we have heard many times and holds at least some truth for me. My husband, Marshall Brodien, and I came to each other from very different life-styles. Marshall's life focus is his magic. He is a magician with more than fifty years of experience. He was an illusionist, stage hypnotist, and starred on the children's television program, "The Bozo Show," as the clown/magician Wizzo. He is a keen businessman and the designer of all Marshall Brodien Magic Company magic products.

My children have been my life's priority. I was a full-time at-home mom for about ten years and then worked around their schedules after that. My career as a writer takes me behind the scenes. I am an observer of people and events. I spend most of my work hours alone doing research and writing.

Marshall is a procrastinator; I am deadline and detail-oriented. He is totally disorganized; I am anally organized. He likes his "stuff" around him; I like clean open spaces. He has been single most of his life; I've been married most of mine. He is street-wise; I am spiritual.

We find each other's gifts and viewpoints complimentary and mentor each other in our areas of expertise. We also share vital similarities. We both are creative, compassionate, and generous. We are enthusiastic about meeting people, seeing different places, and enjoying a variety of activities. Most of all, we truly respect, love, and admire each other.

Having experienced this supportive and mentoring relationship, I am in complete agreement with Cheryl Conover. I know firsthand that the optimum scenario for creating success is to have mentoring relationships at home and at work. Marshall is generous with his support, direction, connections, and opportunity. I am very grateful to have him and his gifts in my life.

Chapter Eight

THE WISDOM OF A MENTOR

The wind propels the sailboat. It influences the speed and direction of the vessel.

Mentors are the wind in your sails. They can accelerate your career voyage. They can guide you down a stream you would never have chosen on your own. You, the sailor, remain in control of the journey. You may choose to resist a mentor's nudge or direction. But as the sailboat does not move without the wind, your progress may be nil or slow without the mentor.

Professional mentors share information they have gained through experience, saving you the time and challenge of discovering the information on your own. They can introduce you to other high-ranking people in your business who have the power to promote and support your growth. They can identify talents and capabilities within you of which you are unaware. They can send you in a direction better suited to your advancement than you otherwise would have chosen.

Attorney Vicky Bush-Joseph said her professional mentor, Ed Butts, sent her in a direction she would not have gone on her own. Ed and Vicky worked at AT&T Telephone Company. Shortly after Ed left AT&T to go to Illinois Bell Telephone Company (now Ameritech), Vicky was put into a position that would have required her to move to New Jersey. The move was not conducive to her family situation and her husband's medical practice. As an alternative, Ed created a unique opportunity for Vicky to join him at Illinois Bell. Vicky gratefully and eagerly accepted the offer.

Vicky said Ed is a wonderful lawyer. She calls on him for practical, concrete advice, because he keeps on top of things. He is proactive; he doesn't wait for things to happen. She also admires the way he treats people and how he acknowledges good work. Vicky said Ed also is aware of the total needs of an employee. He realizes a happy personal life contributes to a successful professional career.

Vicky said when she told Ed she was pregnant with her second child, his first response was that it was not good for her career. His next words were that he was thrilled for her personally. He knew how important it was for her to have the child and that she would be happier overall because of that.

Dr. Monique Anawis changed career direction because of her mentor. Monique's initial medical aspirations were in orthopedics and sports medicine. She understood athletic bumps and bruises from ice-skating. She entered college to pursue a medical degree that would focus on the needs of athletes.

While at Brown University in New England, Monique took a job as an assistant to eye physician Dr. David Walton. There she was exposed to every eye disease, disorder, and correction. She found ophthalmology to be fascinating, in-depth, and technologically progressive. The introduction to Dr. Walton and his medical concentration altered the course in which she followed as a physician.

Monique said she learned from Dr. Walton's extensive knowledge, proficiency, and patient approach. Through his actions, he taught her a sense of humility. She admires his wonderful, kind personality and the way he treats everyone with respect. He is a world expert in childhood glaucoma, yet he remains very humble. Dr. Walton continues to be a strong mentor, role model, and friend to Monique.

Cardiologist Dr. Amy Coene Bales met Dr. John Carroll when she was a resident at the University of Chicago Hospital. She said Dr. Carroll was responsible for interesting her in cardiology and encouraged her to pursue the field. She may not have gone into cardiology without Dr. Carroll's encouragement, and she is grateful she did. Amy said Dr. Carroll was one of those people she felt she could talk to if she had questions through the course of her career. He made her feel important. Amy said she still puts him on a pedestal and goes to him with questions.

Anita Smith, music contractor, was only fifteen years old and had not yet considered any career path when she met her professional mentor. She had been ushering at local theaters and attending classes at Jones Commercial High School. She was recommended by Jones to music contractor and orchestra leader Henry Brandon for a secretarial position. Anita was hired and trained for the position and later as Henry's assistant.

Anita learned every aspect of the business from Henry. She learned how to maintain the accounting books and place the talent in job openings. She accompanied Henry to dance lines, theaters, and orchestras. She was involved in his meetings with unions and openings of concerts, comedians, and musicals. Anita watched how Henry announced acts, produced them, and managed people.

She said she "gained oodles and oodles" of experience from him. Henry was highly respected in the business. He was very fair and honest, and so was she, which is why she felt they made a good team. She said Henry was ageless and adaptable. He was an intuitive, wonderful man. He fit in with people of all walks of life. He could sit in tails at a fancy dinner and talk to a prince or in jeans on a peer and talk with a fisherman.

Anita said Henry mentored her personally as well as professionally. She relied on his wisdom and his kindness. She remembered fondly how he would call her "Neats." She said Henry and her mother, Hilda, were her two most significant influences. "Henry took over where my mother left off. They showed me how to go through life with my eyes open. I feel very fortunate to have had these two people in my life," said Anita.

Spring Boards for Success

Many of The Fabulous Fifty-Two identified their choice of career at a young age. Their sails were set as children and teens. But they acknowledged a powerful force behind them, a mentor, who accelerated and/or enriched, their professional journey. Teresa Orman learned her first skills as a hairstylist in a career-training program in high school nearly twenty years ago. She said what she learned on her first job from her mentor, Judy, could not have been taught in the classroom.

Judy owned a hair styling shop and hired Teresa while she was still in school. She supervised and helped Teresa perfect her techniques. She also shared her business ethics with Teresa. She showed her how to communicate and relate appropriately with other beauticians and clients. Teresa said Judy gave her the confidence to cut hair and work with the customer. She wouldn't have learned what she did without her mentor.

Marcia E. Balestri, geochemist and vice president of the Environmental Technology Development Group at TRW, Inc., formerly BDM International, said her mentors helped her become more professional in her business approach. She said her husband, Bob Balestri, who also is an employee at TRW, helped her develop her skills more rapidly than she could have without him. She also named Art Kubo as an asset to her career. Marcia said Art showed her ways to do things differently than what she came up with on her own. He taught her how to do business on a higher level.

Rev. M. Sue Storm, spiritual and metaphysical advisor and angelic facilitator, said her study in metaphysics was deepened by Genevieve Paulson. Sue said Genevieve taught her about past life regression and how the present lifetime is affected by the past. She taught Sue how to clear the negative effects of a past life from the consciousness, thereby lightening the load in this lifetime.

Psychotherapist Alice Umbach said when everyone around her was telling her to be thankful for the life she had, a counselor she was seeing for marital problems helped her envision a future she could not have seen without him. The counselor encouraged Alice to go after the education and career for which she longed. He offered her the extra push she needed to take the first steps to a completely different life. Alice said that time of her life was exciting but certainly not easy.

Dr. Sue Holstein, clinical psychologist and hypnotherapist, said Susan McCracken, Ph.D. was the first woman she looked to as a role model in her field and one of her strongest professional influences. Sue interned at Lutheran General Hospital under Dr. McCracken.

Sue said Dr. McCracken was generous with her

mentoring time and was very encouraging. She taught Sue to trust her instincts, think for her self, and laugh at herself. She was upbeat and optimistic, always singing and humming. Sue admired Dr. McCracken's client approach and teaching style. She said Dr. McCracken was, and is, astoundingly intuitive. Sue said she has so much respect for her mentor because she is a solid person.

Diana Dionisio-Pieczynski, manager of WGN-TV publicity and promotions, had just graduated college with a major in advertising when she interviewed at WGN-TV. She said she talked her way into Pam Pearson's door and the television station. Because of her inexperience, Diana felt Pam took a chance in hiring her. Yet she taught Diana the nuances of the business. She encouraged her and pushed her. Pam helped Diana set expectations about what could be delivered.

Diana said she continues to find herself quoting Pam's philosophies and calling on her with questions. Diana also names Meagan Bueschel at Tribune Broadcasting as a mentor. She sought Meagan's advice especially in the beginning of her career. She said Meagan continues to guide her in public relations etiquette.

Susan Schreter, president of Caring Products International, said she values the input of mentor Tony (Anthony) Cetrone. Susan worked for Tony several years ago as a financial analyst and consultant. Tony shared stories with her about his past negotiations with Fortune 500 companies and one hundred million dollar contracts. Susan said her business savvy expanded because of what she learned from the situations Tony had encountered, his tactics, and the results of his actions.

Susan said Tony taught her how to achieve her business goals without compromising her integrity. He would tell her the way it was in the real world and how she did not have to be like other people. He pushed her to know the facts, to be well prepared, and not to enter a meeting as an "empty suit." He also taught her the importance of maintaining employee respect.

Tony told Susan how to command attention at a meeting, which is sometimes difficult for women. He suggested she talk with her hands, stand when speaking at meetings while others sit, and even slam a fist on a table to keep their attention. He said sometimes it's all right to be dramatic. He also encouraged her not to be chicken, to stand up for what she believed.

Both Tony and Susan's father suggested that Susan meet guest speakers at presentations - to go to the speaker on a break, introduce herself, and ask detailed questions. Susan said they told her to hang around the "doers."

Judge Hollis Webster said the professionals in her industry were generous with valuable guidance. When she was a partner at the law firm of Hinshaw and Culbertson, the other attorneys in the practice realized her aspirations to become a judge. She said she is not a business person. She never wanted to wine and dine clients, which attorneys must do to build a practice. Her superiors knew she didn't want to remain a partner. Hollis wanted to be a judge. The other attorneys allowed her to grow in her own way.

Hollis said she recognizes Federal Clerk Judge John Norberg for the most significant contribution toward her professional advancement. She was honored when he swore her in as an associate judge. Hollis said he offered her a springboard for a judicial position. He supported her career and how she wanted to combine it with her personal life when she had her children. Hollis said she continues to stay in contact with Judge Norberg.

U. S. Chamber of Commerce Senior Vice President Leslie Wheeler Hortum said she is very blessed in the area of professional mentors. But the journey she took with them was not always smooth. Leslie was hired out of college by Kathleen Parker in the research and development division of the National Chamber Foundation at the United States Chamber of Commerce. Kathleen had great confidence in Leslie, calling her a "rising star." She taught Leslie the ropes of the business and introduced her to Tom Donohue. After Leslie's first year at the chamber, Tom hired her to work in his office.

Three months later, Leslie's road to success hit a pot hole. She and Tom did not get along. In her words, she said he thought she was useless and transferred her to another department. But a few months later, he decided he'd made a mistake and hired her back.

Once Tom got behind Leslie, her upward career movement took a rapid and direct course. Tom gave her lots of opportunity to get involved. She was 22 years old going to meetings and presenting large projects. He encouraged Leslie to make decisions. Tom said if she was right, he would back her up. If she was wrong, they would fix it together.

In 1984 at the age of 25, Tom appointed Leslie Chief Executive Officer of Transport Topics Publishing, a $48.9 million company owned by the American Trucking Association. Tom believed Leslie capable of the challenge and the capacity to learn the necessary details of public affairs, marketing, and the position's responsibilities. Then, when Tom was promoted to Chief Operating Officer, he promoted Leslie to senior vice president and chairmen of the management committee.

In 1997 Tom was appointed President and CEO of the U. S. Chamber of Commerce. Once again he asked Leslie to join him. Leslie was appointed as Senior Vice President for Federation Development. "Tom kept pushing me, challenging me, throwing me into the deep end. There hasn't been a problem I've encountered that we both couldn't figure out together. I am where I am because Tom gave me a chance. He recognized my talent and ability and gave me the opportunity to exercise it," said Leslie.

Daily Doses of Mentoring

If we are lucky, we run across people regularly in our work or home life who contribute to our growth. Jane Hayden, Director of Traffic, WGN Television, counts on National Sales Manager Donald O'Toole to keep a proper perspective of her job. She calls on Donald when she is unsure of the appropriateness of her reactions to situations. Donald is open-minded. She can ask him if she is taking something correctly or blowing it out of proportion. She said he helps her pick and choose her battles and maintain a sense of humor.

Writing is a natural forum for personal and professional development. Everyone I have interviewed for a feature article has taught me something about myself and this world in which we live. As I question an area of life, I research printed resources and interview people with knowledge in that area. I grow because they share a part of themselves with me.

Dr. Monique Anawis said she learns from every doctor, health practitioner, and patient with whom she works. Monique said she gains great insight from one nurse in particular. Nurse Mary Jane is a Native American who was raised on a reservation in Dakota. Her husband is a tribal elder and spiritual leader. Mary Jane combines her Native American medical healing traditions with her advanced medical education. Monique said Mary Jane is a tremendously gifted person. She never loses sight of the benefits of often the simplest cures, such as using chamomile tea compresses for sties.

Patti Doyle Brewer, stockbroker, said the brokers at Solomon Smith Barney, Inc. are very interactive and supportive. They guide and teach each other. If one of them has a question about picking a stock, they watch someone else in the company and learn how they do it. For example Patti said Joe Amonica is helpful overall, Tami Trittschuh is a great technician, Liz Meeker is a source for option information, and Patti's strength lies in her knowledge about bonds. Throughout the day they just wander over to each other's desks and ask for direction when they need it.

Susan Schreter said her Board of Directors often mentor her. Having them available for consultation is very beneficial. They contribute valuable input when considering strategy. She said she trusts this group of people to act as her backbone when making decisions.

Teresa Orman said she learns from talking with her clients. She also learns about her trade from the other stylists. Many beauticians come to her for direction on hair coloring, which is her specialty, and she consults them when she has questions in areas in which they excel. Teresa said most stylists realize the benefits of cooperation and the futility of competition in the industry. She said they have a saying in the business: "There is no need to steal clients. There is plenty of hair to go around."

Mentors for Moments

We are a mobile society. We change our residence, employer, and even career several times in a lifetime. Mentors tend to come and go with these changes. As we make a life-style or professional move, the strengths of a different mentor become more valuable.

Actress Ann Jillian said different mentors were there

for her at different times of her life. At the onset of her career, when Ann was a young child, she had some powerful people behind her. Walt Disney offered Ann her first major role as Little Bo Peep in the movie *Babes in Toyland.* Joyce Sellzman, "the first lady of casting in Hollywood," believed in Ann's potential and offered her opportunity. Entertainer Mickey Rooney was very vocal about endorsing Ann, as well as opening doors, guiding her development, and supporting her progress. Ann said she is thankful for their generous support and their wisdom. "Without a doubt, these mentors made a difference. These earth angels encouraged me and sent me in the right direction," said Ann.

Gerber Plumbing Fixtures Chairman of the Board Harriet Gerber Lewis said she had a mentor when she first took over the business after her father's death. He was the company's accountant. He advised her about the financial end of the business. Harriet said the man was like a second father to her. He was wonderful with finances and explaining the details to her. His guidance helped her to become a better business person.

I've worked with some incredible editors and clients. These short-term mentors gave me the right guidance at the right time. *Chicago Tribune* editors Stephen Lough, Denise Joyce, and Maureen Hart pointed out weak leads, unsubstantiated statements, and libelous verbiage, thereby prompting me to become a better writer. Jim Mozdren, president of Mozdren & Associates, gave me an opportunity in advertising that resulted in an important turn in my career toward significant financial growth. And clients such as Susan Coe Heitsch, Vice President of Corporate Affairs at Bank One, supplied an environment conducive to a higher level of professionalism.

Susan offered me writing projects while I was an employee of Jim Mozdren's advertising and design agency and as an independent contractor. She gave me clear, concise project direction which resulted in my ability to supply her with a high quality product. She acknowledged a job well-done, promoting my self-confidence and ability.

Susan said her mentoring style of working with employees and vendors was due to the caliber of professional mentors she had. These mentors appeared at various times when she needed their guidance and boost to her career. Three of her mentors that particularly stand out are Heather LaRiviere, Charles Spear, and Gordon Koppin.

Heather LaRiviere explained objectives clearly. She coached Susan on the nuances of management and how to partner with employees. She encouraged creative strategy and problem solving. Heather had an MBA decades before it was fashionable. Susan said Heather was her role model for a woman in business. She admired Heather's behavior, professionalism, and vision.

Heather offered Susan tremendous opportunity for advancement. First she moved Susan into a management position from a secretarial job. When she left her position years later, Heather promoted Susan into her spot. Susan said the later promotion was a quantum leap for her career.

Charles Spear offered Susan what she called the opportunity of a life-time. Not only did he double her salary overnight, he helped her hone her professional skills. She said he taught her how to observe people, do leg work to prepare for meetings, and take care of the follow-up. He encouraged forward growth. Susan said working under someone so brilliant was a tremendous asset to her. She learned by just being in Charles Spear's presence.

Susan calls Gordon Koppin "the ultimate mentor." She said mentoring is a part of Gordon's supervisory style. He challenges his employees to do more, to create, and to take on the biggest projects. He contributes to their growth and development by setting quarterly goals and strategizing how to achieve those goals. Susan said working for Gordon was a terrific experience. He gave her his input, then sat back and let her go. Because of this type of mentoring, Susan said she can do what she does in her position today.

She also learned how to handle employee error from Gordon. On one occasion, Susan authorized the use of customer information on mailing envelopes that, she later discovered, if the envelopes had been mailed, could have led to credit card fraud. A million envelopes had to be destroyed, costing the company the envelopes, printing, and time.

"My theory is to tell the truth. Tell the whole truth. And tell it quickly," said Susan. "I went to Gordon and told him what I had printed on the envelopes. He was not happy, but he simply asked if I understood why the language was a problem and if I knew how to fix it. Nothing further was said. There was no yelling or bloodletting. Nothing ever came back to haunt me."

Nurse Debbie McElroy said her professional mentor didn't come into her career until she had been in nursing for four years. After college, she had found a niche where she felt comfortable. She was coordinating home health care for Rush Presbyterian St. Lukes Hospital nearly 20 years ago when home health care was in its infancy. But Debbie said she was seeking a way to incorporate her desire to have a family and advance in her profession.

Debbie met Nurse Ann Crudele at the hospital. She watched Ann blend her people skills and love of her family into her work. Ann had cared for her elderly mother in her home and understood firsthand the rewards and challenges of home health care. She helped Debbie develop a plan to blend her skills with her personal and professional goals.

Debbie said Ann was a hard taskmaster but a good

teacher. Debbie would go to Ann with a plan for a patient, and Ann would point out a different angle and a more complete view of the situation. Ann enhanced her abilities and gave her a clearer perspective. Ann didn't change Debbie's path, but Ann did change her approach to her career.

Dr. Nancy Wilson Dickey, President of the American Medical Association, said her mentors have appeared when she needed to tap into their particular gifts and wisdom. She said many of her mentors were men because there were few women from whom to choose as mentors. That situation is rapidly changing as more women are pursuing medical degrees.

Most overtly, Nancy said Dr. Sam Nixon has mentored her. Dr. Nixon is president of the American Academy of Family Physicians and a skilled mediator. He is a master at identifying, targeting, and solving problems. Nancy said he shares his approach to people and politics and is willing to share his inside strategies.

Nancy said Dr. Benjy Brooks, pediatric surgeon, clearly made an impression on her. She found herself watching Dr. Brooks and how she handled challenging situations. When wondering how to handle a situation today, sometimes Nancy still thinks what course of action Dr. Brook might take.

Nancy said Dr. Isaac Kleinman also influenced her. She met Dr. Kleinman when she was a resident. She said he lived and breathed medicine as it should be done. Nancy watched him juggle multiple demands with ease.

Family physician Dr. Frank Webber was the program director where Nancy trained. Nancy said she admired and learned from his sense of justice and professionalism. Dr. Webber brought equity where there was inequity. He maintained his cool at all times, even when upset. He was a marvelous listener and brings together people with spirit and ideas to find common ground. Nancy called him a superb family physician. She said if she can acquire even a piece of him into her work, she will have peace and serenity.

A young teenager away from home for the first time, Janet Faye Damm said many of the officers reached out to her as a substitute parent, guardian, and mentor when she enlisted in the U. S. Navy. Janet was stationed at Pearl Harbor, Hawaii for three years and San Diego, California for the last year. Some of the officers had daughters her age. They looked after her and took her under their wing. They taught her about responsibility and to think for herself.

Janet said a master chief instructed her on appropriate military behavior and how to relate to other people. A commanding officer and his wife took Janet into their home when she had her tonsils removed. One officer of Japanese descent taught her about the Japanese temperament, how to be more patient, how to handle herself in a business situation, and how to control her emotions. Janet said the officer contributed to her development significantly.

Another officer, Marcia, encouraged Janet to make decisions. She didn't tell Janet what to do or rule out Janet's approach to a problem simply because it was not the usual way to do something. She let her make her own mistakes. She gave Janet the initiative and let her fly with it, which was very good for her self-confidence at 18 and 19 years old. Janet said if she messed up, Marcia would say at least she tried. She'd help her streamline her procedure, see the things she did wrong, and show her how to do it more efficiently the next time.

Professor of Medicine and Director of the Endocrine Research Unit at Mayo Clinic Dr. Cheryl Conover said she thanks many mentors for their contribution to her professional development. Cheryl said Dr. Raymond Hintz at

Stanford, California was very influential. And Dr. Neal Ruderman, her Ph.D. advisor, was her cheerleader. He treated her like a daughter when she worked in his lab.

Dr. Howard Morgan was the physiology department chairperson at Penn State University in Hershey, Pennsylvania when Cheryl was attending graduate school. Cheryl said he mentored her scientifically and emotionally. He understood a young person's concerns about the future. He identified her abilities and offered advice when she needed it.

Dr. George Cahill is the director of Joslin Diabetes Clinic. Cheryl was a technician when Dr. Cahill invited her to play music with his family. Cheryl said he was very kind to her, encouraged her to return to school for her doctorate degree, and mentored her by his exceptional example. She called Dr. Cahill a brilliant scientist and one of our world's leaders in diabetes research. Cheryl said his accomplishments are impressive.

Reflecting on these mentors Cheryl said most mentored for periods of time, although she could call on all of them at any time if she needed advice or a letter of recommendation. Many times they pushed her down paths she would not have taken. She didn't realize how important her mentors were at the time, but she does now, in retrospect. Cheryl said she doesn't know why these mentors had such faith in her or were so interested in promoting her career, but she feels very lucky to have had such wonderful mentoring relationships.

No Limits for Women Artists workshop leader Debra Trent said Kathy Hickock, the director of women's studies at Iowa State University, paved a path for her when Kathy asked her to join the Committee for Women's Studies. Debra said Kathy created possibilities for her she had never imagined. She showed her how to branch out and explore.

Debra said her professional projection was broadened also because of environmental artist Betsy Damon. Debra said she had limited her professional dreams before meeting Betsy because of her own lack of vision. Coming from a lower economic status, Debra said she had been socialized to believe great success in the arts to be impossible for her. Together Debra and Betsy grew to understand life from opposing viewpoints.

"Betsy is someone who has reached across so many different barriers," said Debra. "She has mentored me in excellent ways. She has helped me to believe in myself and set goals at a level I never dreamed of. Our relationship is a fine example of how well diversity can work."

Carole Miller said when she was appointed principal of a boys correctional facility, two of her bosses helped her incorporate her past experience as a special education coordinator and her own standard of ethics into her supervisory role. Carole learned by watching her mentors and through their on-going guidance. She said they operated with integrity and taught her how to use, rather than abuse, power.

Carole said she has total respect for her mentors. They gave her an understanding of how one should behave in a position of authority. She learned from them how to formulate a workable modus operandi, a standard of values that was in harmony with her own. She said she would have struggled longer without them.

On the first day Carole took a tour of state facilities, she told an employee one of her goals was to make him smile. She saw a sadness in the man she wanted to help lighten. In response to Carole's remark, the employee filed a harassment complaint with the union. Carole knew she had not acted inappropriately but felt a sense of failure at the onset of her job. She consulted her mentor who told her how to deal with the complaint. He also told her to look at the big picture and continue on with her work. "In his folksy down-to-earth way, he said in a hundred years none of it would matter," she said.

Carole said through these mentors she learned how to deal with administrators and staff who were typically more challenging than the students. She said she was often discriminated against and threatened by other employees, because she would not tolerate them treating students unkindly. She did not allow them to use four letter words or demeaning language with students. Both of Carole's mentors were highly educated and extremely articulate. They supported her efforts and offered concrete direction under the most difficult circumstances.

Astrologer Barbara Junceau said she recognizes many individuals who have mentored her in her field. Barbara said she models how she handles people after Barbara Bacon, a former boss. She said she learns from the way Robert Schmidt, an astrologer, philosopher, mathematician, and linguist, pulls astrological information together in a reasonable way and clearly demonstrates why and how astrology works. She said she respects Astrologer Ann Parker's professional caliber and support. She credits Ann for encouraging her to write her first book and begin lecturing at conferences.

Barbara also values Donna Van Toen as a strong supporter, who put her own money behind some of the conferences in which Barbara has participated as a speaker.

Alan Oken, a brilliant esoteric teacher/healer who speaks seven languages, sat down and shared his material on soul centered astrology with a small group of astrologers that included Barbara. He introduced her to the astrological mystery traditions. Barbara said he had a profound impact on her thinking. She felt privileged and exceedingly grateful for his guidance and friendship.

Pamela Sullivan, senior vice-president of TRW, Inc.,

counts two individuals as professional mentors. Pamela said discrimination was not supposed to be tolerated, but it did exist toward the few women employees at the beginning of her career. She was questioned at the job interview about her plans to have children and was hired for $3,000 less than her male counterparts. Jim Schwarz was more open-minded than most of the other managers. He recognized her potential and encouraged her professional advancement. As time went on Pamela said Jim grew to believe in her competence and gave her more and more difficult assignments.

Another manager Pamela names as a mentor was Dr. Joseph Braddock. Joe was one of the company founders and very influential. She said Joe was good for her and she for him. He sent her on an exciting path. He was a risk taker, and she was a risk taker, so she felt supported in taking risks. Pamela said she always considered Joe in her corner.

Alice Umbach, psychotherapist, said an important mentor of hers lived next door when she was a child. Neighbor Esther Philips offered her a perspective unlike anyone else in her life. Esther originally was very wealthy with servants and finery. Then her husband went through some severe financial losses and her life-style made a turnabout. Esther took control of her husband's business, and became the brains of the company. But as a business woman in the 1940s, however Esther took a back seat to the other men. In spite of these challenges and financial losses, Alice said Esther assumed her change in status and life-style with grace and dignity.

Esther was different from other women Alice knew. Esther ate dinner by candlelight. She talked to Alice about her philosophy of life, how she should never buy a washing machine — she should send her laundry out. Esther was an incredible dresser and entertainer. She coordinated fabulous parties.

Alice said Esther also was very generous. She loaned money to several poor families in the area without keeping any written records. She let farm workers live in houses on the property when they couldn't afford to live on their own. Alice said Esther was her role model for working women. She patterned her life-style after her, and continues to have so much admiration for her.

Pearls of Wisdom

Adding a pearl necklace to a plain sheath or tank dress enhances the total grace of the outfit and the wearer. Pearl necklaces are particularly elegant and adorn the dress unlike any other type of jewelry. Looking individually at the pearls, we find each to be unique and lovely. Linked together, the pearls combine into a precious piece of jewelry.

Several of The Fabulous Fifty-Two are connected in much the same way as those pearls. Each is special and plays an important role in contributing to the development of the benefactor. Linked together they enhance each other's strength and beauty.

In a previous chapter, Nurse Debbie McElroy named Ingrid Sharos, Adult Probations Supervisor, as her peer mentor. Both Debbie and Ingrid have other mentors and mentor other people, but they are better, happier, and stronger because of the relationship they share.

Patti Doyle Brewer added Sue Darby, First Vice President of Solomon Smith Barney, to her list of mentors. Patti has 15 years of experience in the stock market. Few women were in the business when she began her career, so Patti was grateful to have Sue available to her as an experienced woman in the business.

Marcia Balestri said she is connected to TRW Senior Vice President Pamela J. Sullivan. Marcia said Pamela is a very positive role model and influence on her. She said she admires Pamela and her work style.

Judy Chaffe, a self-employed personnel trainer for Chrysler Corporation, said she learned by watching and observing Marlene Tighe. At the time Judy met Marlene, Marlene was an area operations manager for Ohio Bell Telephone Company. Judy said Marlene was a phenomenal manager with her people. She could identify a customer's attitude and personality and respond quickly to that customer in a way that was needed.

Guided Imagery and Music Therapist Louise Dimiceli-Mitran is connected to Dr. Helen Bonny, the developer of GIM. The intensive training program to become a Bonny Foundation therapist includes pairing with at least one foundation certified therapist for three years. Louise selected Helen as her mentor. All of Louise's sessions are reported to Helen. Helen regularly advises and guides Louise in her growth and development as a therapist.

Helen studied the affects of inducing altered states of consciousness with music and LSD in a government funded program at the Maryland Psychiatric Institution. When LSD was outlawed, she continued the study using only music. She found the therapeutic affects of particular music played in particular ways to be significant. Romantic composers such as Beethoven, Brahms, Tchaikovsky, Mozart, and Schumann could raise emotions and imagery deep within the subconscious. Helen pioneered the GIM program based on some of the results of her studies.

Today there are GIM training centers across the U.S. and in Australia, Denmark, Norway, Sweden, New Zealand, the United Kingdom, Germany, and Switzerland. Helen oversees the progress of all students and fellows in the GIM program. She is highly respected as the GIM creator and Bonny Foundation founder.

Emily K. Emmerman, Vice President of Strategic Services at University of Chicago Hospitals and Health System, said her professional mentor is Ruth Chodak, Vice President of Business Development. Ruth hired Emily, opened doors for her, and guided her advancement and growth. She met with Emily on a regular basis. She helped her develop skills she didn't have. Ruth gave Emily experience in making board presentations. She helped her project best/worst case scenarios and how she could respond. Ruth even prepared Emily to take over her job when she moved out of it.

Emily said Ruth lobbied for her and hired her for a position she would not have been considered for by anyone else. She laid out a road map through the political waters for her to follow. She taught her to use her instincts. She tutored her and educated her.

Emily said their relationship is friendly as well as professional. There is a magnetism that exists between them. Ruth acknowledges Emily as a complete person and not just an employee. She advises her on how to balance work and family responsibilities - how to allow necessary time with her son without compromising her professional position. When Emily wanted to work four-day work weeks, she was told it could not be done in her position. Emily went back to Ruth who strategized and pulled a working plan together.

"Ruth has a powerful influence over me. She built my confidence. I'm very thankful to have had her support. She gave me the opportunity. Now it's up to me to live up to her expectations," said Emily.

An example of a longer string of mentors begins with my association with Rev. M. Sue Storm and continues with Sue's association with Alice Umbach. I interviewed many of Sue's clients when I wrote a feature article on her for the *Chicago Tribune*. The clients told me how Sue mentors and empowers them. I too have been empowered by her. Sue has taught me, as her clients told me she taught them, how to envision, create, and fulfill a prosperous, happy life for myself.

Sue said she is able to mentor like that because of Alice Umbach, her mentor and counselor. She said Alice is caring and insightful. She is available for guidance when no other human being is. She is like a second mother to her. Sue said Alice accelerates her growth through loving support and concrete information. She reframed her thinking to be more productive. She gently shifted her thought process. Alice helped her make necessary changes in herself more easily than she would have done on her own. She gave her the strength to explore her potential. Sue said Alice made an absolute and positive difference in her life.

All men by nature desire knowledge.

Aristotle, *Metaphysics, bk. I, ch. 1*

Chapter Nine

DIVINE GUIDANCE

In recognizing the mentors in the lives of The Fabulous Fifty-Two, several women named those whom exist other than on the physical plane. Actress Ann Jillian said she calls on the heavens when she needs assistance. She said God, Jesus Christ, and His mother, Mary, are all her mentors. Ann believes she receives solid answers to her prayers from these sources.

Susan Coe Heitsch, Bank One's Vice President of Corporate Affairs, said she relies on the written word from God to man. She looks to the Bible, and especially the Ten Commandments, as blueprints for how she should live her life. She said she finds straight-forward information in the Bible. When she needs an answer to something, Susan reads the Bible. She said her answer can be found there.

Assistance doesn't only come from God. It can also come from Him indirectly. General Practitioner Dr. Ruth Martens said when she needs help someone always seems to come forward. Ruth said she never feels like she is on her own. It is as if people "drop from the sky" whenever she needs them. Ruth added that when earthly beings aren't available, heavenly ones are. "I must have a team of guardian angels on my side. Disasters come right and left and I still survive," she said.

PMS educator Linaya Hahn said she gets her guidance from what she simply calls the divine. She feels she is led in certain directions by a higher power. "I don't know where I will be led in six months or the next year. I just feel honored to be in the position I am in. Life is very exciting and so much fun," Linaya said.

Spiritual Development

I was born on May 31, 1954 in Chicago, Illinois. My parents, older brother, Mike (John Michael), and I lived in a one-bedroom apartment on the edge of the Mundelien College and Loyola University campuses where my parents attended school. Many of my parents' friends were nuns and priests who were teachers or advisors at those schools. They would come to our home, or we would visit them at the convent, rectory, or campus.

The priest who baptized me, Very Rev. Fr. Clement M. O'Donnell, OFM, was one of my father's professors at Loyola. Father Clem was later transferred to the Vatican, St. Peter's Basilica in Rome, Italy. I exchanged letters with Father Clem from the time I was about six years old until his death some twenty years later. Father Clem also stayed with us two weeks each summer. During that period my family would go with Father to the seminary to visit his priest-friends. Father taught me a reverence for the Catholic Church. Through him I was shown examples of how it was to be a keeper, administrator, and teacher of our faith.

After my sister, Patti, was born, we moved to a larger

three-bedroom apartment across the street from Our Lady of the Angels Church. I attended Our Lady of the Angels school from first to sixth grade. Sometimes my father would work at the convent, and I would go with him. I loved the BVM (Blessed Virgin Mary) nuns. They taught me about my faith and how to pray the rosary. Even as a young child, it was not unusual for me to go into the church to pray alone.

My parents talk and live the Catholic faith. Prayer is a part of our everyday family life. Often times parties with extended family members begin with a mass. We either meet at a church or ask a priest to say a mass for us at special birthdays and celebrations. I continue to enjoy spiritual discussions with friends, family, and my pastor, Father Joseph Jarmoluk.

I went to a public junior high and high school in Oak Park, Illinois where I had some exposure to other religions. But my Catholic faith was never really challenged until I worked at *Spotlight*, an Indian and Pakistani newspaper. I learned about the many Indian religions including Hindu, Moslem, Christian, Zoastrian, and Sikh, while writing feature articles for that paper. From 1991 through 1994, I wrote features for the *Chicago Tribune*. Many of the feature articles I wrote for that publication related to alternative beliefs. Then I was hired at Mozdren & Assoc., a Christian advertising and design agency. Christianity from a Protestant perspective was often discussed between employees there.

I also attended Judson College, a Baptist school, where I received my Bachelor of Arts Degree in Business Management and Leadership in 1997. Christianity was brought into every subject taught and many professors, such as Dr. Lester Hirst, reached out as friends and spiritual advisors as well as teachers.

Applying the Spiritual Connection

So, now you are asking what all of this has to do with mentoring. I give you my background to point out the tremendous number of religious influences in my life. I have had dozens of spiritual mentors. My beliefs are not identical to theirs. In fact, I completely disagree with some of their teachings. But I have learned from all of them. Most importantly, these earthly mentors led me to powerful heavenly mentors.

Spirituality is an integral dimension of my being, and I am very grateful for that. I believe in God and His omnipotent power. He is my greatest mentor. I ask. He answers. When I need guidance, I pray and then listen and watch for the direction in which to follow.

Sometimes the answers to my prayers seem miraculous to me. When my mother was diagnosed with multiple myeloma, the doctors said she would live only six weeks. She lived nearly three years beyond that diagnosis. She even had some very strong, healthy, and happy periods of time. My family believes we prayed my mother's illness into periods of remission.

Our belief in the power of prayer in health and recovery is not unfounded. Research is showing that people who pray and have strong spiritual beliefs live longer and healthier lives. Authors Bernie S. Siegel, M.D. of *Love, Medicine & Miracles* and Larry Dossey, M.D. of *Healing Words* write about the positive affects of prayer on their patients' recovery from major illnesses. Dr. Dossey stated in his book that it didn't seem to matter to which religion people belonged or how they prayed. What did matter was that they did pray or were prayed for while sick.

According to the October 12, 1998 issue of *Time* magazine, a recent study conducted by Duke coincides with this finding. Duke followed 30 patients in a catheter lab at the

Durham VA hospital. Results showed that patients who were prayed over by strangers were 50% to 100% better than those of a control group. Although the study group was done on a small scale, the fact that the study was made shows the medical profession's interest in prayer healing and the great possibility of its benefits in coordination with traditional medical practices.

Of course, asking for recovery from illness is not the only form of prayer. Prayer can be for adoration, repentance, or any plea for assistance. Divine guidance is a form of mentoring as a result of prayer to an unearthly source. When one prays or connects to this source, direction is believed to be given and opportunities present themselves which were previously unavailable to the person praying. I call this source God. Some people call it the spirit, the universe, the Great Spirit, or a higher power.

Passing on the Spirit

My prayers are that I do God's work in God's way. More than half of The Fabulous Fifty-Two made similar statements to me saying they pray for their work to be spiritually driven. Barbara Junceau is a professional astrologer and personal and spiritual counselor. She has a Masters Degree in Theology from Andover Newton Theological School in Massachusetts. She encourages her clients to consider their spiritual growth when questioning physical concerns. Barbara said that students come to her classes and office, because they wish to be involved in their own development. They want to become the best person they can be.

Barbara uses astrology to assist clients in gaining a better understanding of their personalities, talents, intellect, spirituality, relationships, and professional potential.

Barbara said the astrological birth chart, a chart derived from the time, date, and location of birth, is her greatest tool. It is a unique document that reveals so much about an individual in a non-judgmental way. Barbara calls this chart the blueprint of a lifetime.

Barbara began her astrological studies under Goswami Kriyananda at the Temple of Kriya Yoga. She said his teachings had an impact on her. Often as a question arises as to how to counsel a client, Barbara said she refers to the teachings of several individuals, one of which is Goswami Kriyananda. She called his extraordinary spiritual wisdom "phenomenal."

Reverend M. Sue Storm is the founder of Angelight Productions, a spiritual advisor and angelic facilitator. Sue said she relates messages from angels to clients in private and group settings and helps people connect with their personal angels. She is considered a spiritual mentor to many of her clients.

Sue said she receives her own spiritual mentoring from the angels. She asks them for guidance and hears their response. She also consults an earthly source, Rev. Carol Canova, for spiritual mentoring. Sue said Carol was the first person to realize her talents and point her in a more spiritual direction. She gives her practical and loving advice in a very gentle but powerful and effective way. Carol took Sue on as a student and never failed to be available, to teach, guide, and encourage her.

Dr. Helen Bonny, the founder of GIM (Guided Imagery and Music), shared a story on how her life-focus was changed after a spiritual event more than 48 years ago. At the time, she already had a spiritual basis. She was a minister's wife. She also was, and still is, a violinist.

Helen was in her church rehearsing a violin piece for the evening epiphany service. The guest speaker, Dr. Frank Laubach, stood in the wings waiting to practice his own oral presentation. Hearing Helen's rehearsal, Dr. Laubach was moved by her ethereal rendition. Dr. Laubach told Helen that he believed God spoke through her violin.

That evening when Helen performed for the congregation, she said the music was unlike anything she had ever played to that point in time or has ever played since. She believed the perfect, pure, soul-wrenching music to have been heaven-sent. "I knew I couldn't have played it myself," said Helen. "The experience was very profound. The direction of my life changed completely with that one moment in time."

By sharing that awesome experience with Dr. Laubach, a bond was formed between the two. Helen attended Dr. Laubach's workshops and kept in contact with him until his death. She credits him for inspiring her to opening her talent to a spiritual direction. Helen calls Dr. Laubach the father of the work she does at GIM.

Spiritual mentors teach protégés how to connect with spiritual beings and teachings. These protégés often turn around to mentor other protégés to do the same. Fox Valley Christian Church volunteer Sandy Oler is studying to be a discussion leader for her church's Bible study groups. She works with a mentor in preparing responses to anticipated questions. Sandy is learning how to teach other women how to study the Bible on their own.

Sandy said that her discussion leader, Laurie, and two other mentors, Kim and Sherry, have taken her to a spiritual level she would not have gone without them. She said they excite women about learning the Bible. Sandy added that she follows Sherry's footsteps by leading many of the committees Sherry had led the previous year. She is not intimidated by those jobs after watching Sherry. Sandy said she wants to be a leader like Sherry is and what better way to learn how to become that type of leader than from Sherry herself.

Susan Coe Heitsch and hair stylist Teresa Orman both said they wish they could be more open about their Christian beliefs while at work. But with freedom of religion to the general public comes some religious restrictions on a personal level. They said their Christian work ethics must be underlying in their work but not overt. Teresa said her compassion and code of confidentiality with the private information clients share with her when they sit in her solon are based on her Christian beliefs. Susan said much the same. She must respect other religions. However, without mentioning her own beliefs, she can set a Christian example in the way she works with people.

Spirit-Centered Lives

From the time Sister Mary Stella Schellenberger entered the Catholic order, Servants of the Holy Heart of Mary, in 1949 she has devoted her life to God. Her faith is incorporated in every factor of her life. She dresses, lives, works, and thinks as a Catholic nun.

Her dual objective is to maintain her connection to God and assist others in their spiritual development. Sister Mary Stella was stationed at a girls' boarding school in Moments, Illinois for eight years. She mothered and nurtured the young people in residence. From 1972 to 1998 she was the Religious Education Director for St. Peter Church in Geneva, Illinois. She oversaw the instruction of more than one hundred adults and 800 children attending St. Peter's religious classes in 1998 alone. She said her goal was to be present for the students and to empower them until her retirement at the end of the 1997-1998 school year.

Sister Mary Stella said her mentors appeared at times in her life when she needed a bridge. They were people who took her from one point to the next. She grew up in Indiana, the oldest of six children in her family. She had wonderful, supportive relationships with her parents, siblings, grandparents, aunts, and uncles. Several other family members also joined religious orders.

Sister Mary Stella's circle of support expanded when she joined the convent. Regardless of age or level, they helped one another. There was a lot of warmth and sharing. Sister Mary Stella said they could go to the superior or anyone else in the (religious) community for help. If they still couldn't find answers, their superior would help them find someone outside the community.

When Sister Mary Stella entered the convent nearly fifty years ago, she was in daily contact with a large number of other religious people. But about half way into her vocation, the number of nuns and priests rapidly dwindled. Those built-in mentors with whom she identified now are far and few between. The only advantage to this scenario is that she lives and intermingles more like a devout Christian lay-person today than in the past. Sister Mary Stella looks to her spiritual director, priests, co-workers, friends, and lay-people for guidance. Now she can relate to them as she could not have in the past.

Rabbi Deborah Zecher oversees the spiritual direction of the congregation at Hevreh of Southern Berkshire, a reform congregation and Union of American Hebrew Congregations in Great Barrington, Massachusetts. Her religious mentoring experience is almost the opposite of Sister Mary Stella's. As the number of peers dwindle for Sister Mary Stella, Deborah's increase.

Women have been allowed ordination into the Jewish faith since 1972. When Deborah was ordained in 1982, few female rabbis were available to observe. Today, there are approximately 300 reform women rabbis in this country out of a total of 1600. And the ratio of men to women coming out of the seminary continues to reverse. At least as many female as male rabbis are now being ordained each year.

Although Deborah recognizes many role models and mentors, initially it was nearly impossible to find one to whom she could completely identify. Being a mentor to other rabbis and seeking a rabbi to mentor her is different than mentors of other professions because her religion is an integral element in every facet of her life. She is a Jewish rabbi, Jewish wife, Jewish mother, Jewish neighbor, and so on.

Also, Deborah said traditionally a rabbi's success is measured in relation to the size of the congregation to which she is responsible. She does not consider that guideline in determining her own success, because she has other considerations, such as her marriage and three children, which are no less important to her. Only another female rabbi can truly relate to many of the questions she had in the early years of her vocation.

The first ordained female rabbi, Sally Priesand, was not a role model for Deborah until recently. Rabbi Priesand was 26 years old when she was ordained. The media thrust her into the role as model for women who wanted to be a rabbi. Initially, Deborah did not agree with Rabbi Priesand's approach. As the years have gone by, Deborah has come to understand Rabbi Priesand more clearly.

Deborah said she did not want to make Rabbi Priesand's path as hers. Her career choices were very different. But now Deborah has gained a profound appreciation for this woman. She respects the decisions Rabbi Priesand has made. Deborah said, "I realize she did not want to be a role model. She only wanted to work in her calling. She wanted to honor Judaism. As a result, she has grown into her role as a model for women rabbis with such grace."

Rabbi Jason Edelstein was Deborah's neighbor when she was a child. One time when he needed someone to take a leadership position in the congregation, Deborah came forward. "Rabbi Edelstein didn't say I couldn't do it, that I was only a child. He encouraged me. He allowed me to take on other positions. He also was affirming when I decided to be a rabbi," she said. Deborah said she treasures the influence Rabbi Edelstein had on her life. She admires his purity to Judaism and models his religious conviction, but not his approach, because their personalities are so different. Deborah said Rabbi Edelstein is tall, austere, and dignified. He is very thoughtful and reflective. She is loud and funny.

Rabbi Lawrence Hoffman was another important mentor to Deborah. Rabbi Hoffman was her professor at rabbinic school. Deborah said he taught her how to be a rabbi. She felt comfortable asking him any question at any time because Dr. Hoffman was never judgmental. He was observant, encouraging, affirming, and supportive.

She also credits Rabbi Jack Stern for her spiritual and vocational development. Deborah was the first woman rabbi to come to Rabbi Stern's congregation. From the very beginning, Rabbi Stern accepted Deborah as his colleague. He freely shared his experience and wisdom with his protégé.

Deborah said Rabbi Stern was an important mentor in the traditional sense. They met regularly to discuss her progress, the basics of the job, theology, and any struggles she was facing.

A great flame follows a little spark.

Dante Alighieri
Ibid. I. 34

Chapter Ten

TRAIL BLAZERS

In the poem "The Road Not Taken" Robert Frost wrote about choosing between a path that many people have walked before and one few have taken. By choice or default, many of us are blazing new trails because at least to some extent, the tried and true ones no longer exist.

Pioneers treading these new roads require a strong sense of courage. Dr. Nancy Wilson Dickey is the first woman to attain the position of president in the American Medical Association. She said being on the forefront can be very stressful. It is easier to follow any path that has been trodden before than to be the one who leads the way.

Today's world is like no other in history. The global environment is complicated, intricate, interwoven, technical, and continuously and rapidly evolving. The use of computers in every industry is giving birth to an extensive list of new jobs.

Job descriptions of many careers are very different than even ten years ago. These changes require new skills and abilities. Industries such as graphic arts and architecture are a fine example. Not long ago, designs were done by hand on drafting tables. Today they are created on the computer. If an artist or architect does not have considerable knowledge of the sophisticated computer programs, finding a job in these fields is nearly impossible.

Women entering the work force after many years as full-time homemakers face additional issues. They may be uncertain of their skill level, how to attain the necessary training or education to raise that level, or even know the direction they wish to pursue. Being out of the work force for an extended period of time, their self-esteem is usually at a low point. The idea of playing hard ball with the big guys can be intimidating.

Carol Havey's book, *Women and Self-Confidence*, and the seminars she presented to groups around the country targeted these issues. She wrote the book as a form of mentorship, reaching out to women in transition. Carol wanted to help raise their self-esteem and find answers to the questions above. She also promoted some practical business skills such as how to network, interview, and dress for success.

Carol also assists participants at her seminars with the three key steps to decision-making. She said those steps are:

1. Figure out what you really want.
2. Consider what it will take to get what you want; and finally,
3. Decide if you are willing to pay the price for what you want.

Carol said that everything comes with a price whether it be in time or energy or whatever. But if you are willing to make the commitment, then don't let anyone slow you down. There always will be people to tell you what you can't do. Don't take "No" for an answer.

Not Just for Men Anymore

Many of The Fabulous Fifty-Two can be considered pioneers who ventured into traditionally male territory. I asked these women how they were treated by the male foundation. I was surprised and delighted to hear so many positive stories of male mentors who freely shared wisdom, direction, networks, and support.

Marcia Balestri, geochemist and vice president of the Environmental Technology Development Group at TRW, said the men in her field were very helpful to her. It's not easy to get to the top without help and she was fortunate to have several mentors who helped her immensely. Marcia said she is very appreciative of the interest they took in her career.

Harriet Gerber Lewis always has been actively involved in many groups and in the plumbing fixture business. She said she is comfortable working with men or women and was never treated any differently than anyone else when she worked with mostly men. She said she was recognized purely on her merit, not gender.

Many years ago Ruby Frank was employed at National Container Corporation. She worked with several Jewish men who taught her a great deal about business. World War II was going on and women were needed in the work force. The business arena was very appealing to Ruby. She saw a challenge and met that challenge. She reached a level in the company no other woman before her had achieved.

Ruby said the men with whom she worked appreciated her talent, ambition, and dedication. They gave her opportunity to advance, succeed, and fly. They taught her to network, the importance of attending meetings, and how to make her presence in business known. She credited those men for being good teachers.

Even five years ago, Pamela Sullivan said there were hardly any other women in her company, TRW, formerly called BDM. She was the highest-ranking woman, and therefore had no other women to go to for mentoring. Pamela said the men who mentored her were very helpful, and she saw no difference in learning the business from a man than if a woman mentor was available.

Women are still a minority in the judicial system, but the ratio of men to women is evening out and is projected to continue to do so. Traditionally judges are sworn in at the end of their law careers. The Honorable Hollis Webster was sworn in as a judge at the age of 34 years old. She said she never encountered any gender bias or deterrents for seeking the position at such a young age. Opportunities were open to her as any one else of any age or gender in the field.

Hollis recommends more women consider judicial positions as a career path. She said women bring a special quality to the bench. The job is suited to the female temperament. Where attorneys must be aggressive in the trenches, judges must be fair, just, and good listeners - qualities that come naturally to women. In addition, the daytime hours required at the bench are easier to balance with motherhood than the nights and weekends that must be worked as an attorney.

Rabbi Deborah Zecher was also a pioneer in her field. She was one of the first women rabbis. She said women are entering that field in unprecedented numbers, also. Deborah participates in a woman's rabbinic mentoring network, which had not previously been available to her. Deborah said she is eager to share her knowledge from 15 years of experience as a rabbi. Although male rabbis have been very generous mentors, she appreciates having other women rabbis from the network with whom she can mentor and consult. Deborah said she thinks her participation in the organization is very important for her and those she talks to, because the mentoring occurs in both directions. She said they learn from their variety of life paths.

Dr. Cheryl Conover said she has flourished at the Mayo Clinic because her superiors were very supportive of her career there. No one ever told her she could not do something because she was a woman. But she said she also did not look for discrimination. She did not carry a chip on her shoulder. Cheryl said she related to her superiors and fellow employees with respect and they treated her the same way in return.

Cheryl said, in retrospect, she realizes how fortunate she is to have had wonderful mentors who gave so much of themselves to her. She was not always certain about her path. Sometimes her mentors pushed her in directions she did not feel confident to take. They recognized her potential, encouraged, directed, and supported her growth so much more than she could have done for herself.

They also taught her about the significance of ethics in a competitive environment. She said her mentors are excellent scientists with the highest ethics. They taught her that back-stabbing is not necessary to get ahead and that she does not have to compromise herself in any way for success.

Kathleen Freeland said she came across some discrimination at the onset of her career in horticulture but also had some dynamic men behind her. She was born in South Dakota and traveled all over the world, moving every three years because of her husband's work. She had two small children in school when a friend took her to a garden club meeting. She joined the club and found becoming a member to be a way to meet other people from different walks of life, different cultures, and different ideas but with similar interests. She enjoyed the camaraderie between members and the stability the club offered in her ever-changing life-style. Wherever her next move took her, there was another garden club to be found.

Kathleen went to Weston Nurseries in Massachusetts in 1970 to interview for a position as a writer with their magazine. She got the job and moved into horticulture as a propagator within her first year there. She was 30 years old, a good age to enter the business, according to Kathleen.

Kathleen said she was one of four women out of 1800 people in the field at that time. Her presence was treated with scrutiny by most. Kathleen said it was all right for women to participate in the garden club. Entering in the field as a paid professional was another issue. Her persistence in pursuing horticulture as a career path helped to permanently change those attitudes.

One very influential mentor and supporter of her career was Edmund Mezitt. Edmund was president of Weston Nurseries, and Kathleen worked closely with him. Edmund was a big name in horticulture. Kathleen said he taught her everything he knew, introduced her to the top people in the business, and gave her responsibilities from which to learn and grow. In exchange, Kathleen became his right arm. Edmund died 15 years ago, but Kathleen said she still carries his picture in her wallet.

Another important mentor was Ralph Shugert. Now in his seventies, Kathleen said Ralph is still active in horticulture. He is a powerful player in the field and known to some as the Father of Propagation. Kathleen said his mentoring was vital to her success. He was one of her best supporters and most knowledgeable advisors. "We need a lot of Ralphs in this world," Kathleen said. "I wouldn't be where I am without Ralph or my other mentors."

Susan Schreter, the President and Co-founder of Caring Products International, designed, patented, and marketed the company's products which are sold in national chains such as Osco and Walgreen Drug Stores. Caring Products was selected by NASA for use by astronauts and test pilots to wear under space suits.

Susan claims her level of success to be partially the result of a strong, independent background and early exposure to the manufacturing setting. She said women are typically reluctant to venture into starting a business from scratch. Those who do usually don't know much about building a company. They have an idea for an outstanding product, but not how to manufacture the product and run the business. Being one of the first women in manufacturing, she tries to be available for other women interested in her work.

Like most of the women above, First Vice President of Solomon Smith Barney Sue Darby said she did not come across any discrimination from peers, superiors, or clients in the 36 years she has been in her field, either. Some male clients even preferred to work with her because she was a woman.

Sue's trailblazing in the male world of the stock market was not a conscious decision she had thought about from childhood but rather one she stumbled upon after college graduation. She had majored in English in college, which she said prepared her to do nothing. She moved to San Francisco after graduation because she thought it was an exciting town. She then looked for a job where she could meet a lot of men. She ran into a friend who was working for a brokerage firm and was told the field was exciting and definitely male-dominated.

Sue said she is not a mathematical or research type person and didn't know anything about the stock market, but she did enjoy talking on the telephone and the people aspect of the job. She decided that was the job she wanted, interviewed with Paine Webber, studied for the exam, scored the highest grade ever previously recorded on the test, and started her career as a broker. Sue said when you are determined, you can do anything you want to do. That's what America's all about.

Sue said San Francisco was a wonderful, fun place in the 1960s. There was so much to do and great places to eat. Mornings were busy with the market, but when it closed at 12:30 PM she had the afternoon to listen to the Grateful Dead, drink Irish coffee, see the upcoming Phyllis Diller in coffee houses like the Purple Onion and the Hungry Eye, and sit on porches looking at the flowers.

At that time the stock market was pretty straight-forward. There were few mutual funds and no index funds. And the general public was not involved in it. Sue said only the wealthy were in the stock market then. Today even children talk about it.

Women brokers were far and few between but, surprisingly, Sue did encounter one woman broker who helped her very much. Mentor Pat Howe was in the bond business with the firm L. F. Rothchild when Sue started with Pain Webber. She taught Sue how to handle her business, what to buy, and freely passed on information to her. She helped Sue to learn and understand her accounts. Pat's strong presence as a successful woman in the stock market encouraged Sue to find her own success. Sue said she learned so much about the business because of Pat's generous time and introduction to the field. Mentors like her are difficult to find in her competitive business. Sue said she continues to maintain contact with Pat. In addition to a dynamic role model, teacher, and friend, Pat is now Sue's client. She said Pat is a terrific and very unique individual.

Sue left San Francisco nearly 30 years ago when her mother, who was living in Wisconsin, became very ill. She got a job with another firm that was later bought out by

Smith Barney, which is now Solomon Smith Barney. In return for the mentoring she received, Sue said she helps any stockbroker who comes to her. She eagerly shares her experience and knowledge. She said she would help anyone with anything except to give her clients away.

Jumping Hurdles

Like anyone traveling down new paths, The Fabulous Fifty-Two pioneers have encountered a variety of hurdles. Emily Emmerman said being young and petite in her position, she strives to have superiors take her seriously. She has not faced any sexual discrimination but does see many older male superiors looking to her like a daughter. She appreciates their sensitivity but does not want them to lose sight of her capabilities.

Judy Chaffee, professional training consultant and public speaker, found her challenge in being taken seriously by financial institutions. In 1983 she looked for financing to start her first company. She went to seven banks to get a line of credit for J&J Communications. She was looking for the minimum level of financing and showed a comprehensive business plan. Judy and her partner were turned down seven times, because they were told they must have a husband's signature on the loan.

J&J Communications was opened without the assistance of a bank. The projected plan was to achieve a half million dollars in sales by year five. That goal was accomplished in two years. Several years later, Judy was speaking to a group about her business success. After the presentation a woman from the audience approached her and said she was one of the bankers who had turned her down for financing. The woman apologized to Judy for not believing in J&J's potential.

Dr. Jeannette Martens Sorrentino looked for respect in the classroom when she attended dental school. There were 30 women in a class of 160. During slide presentations it wasn't unusual for photos of women in provocative poses to be interspersed between biological slides. Most often, Jeannette said nothing. One time she went into the dean's office to make a complaint about her valuable class time being spent on demeaning and rude material. Jeannette said that type of inappropriate behavior is no longer allowed.

Solomon Smith Barney Second Vice President Patti Brewer said no one can stand in the way of a broker's success. When she got her license 15 years ago, she felt positions were available to her as a woman as often as they were for men. After that, it was up to her to acquire and maintain a clientele and possess the knowledge, understanding, and instincts necessary in the market. Patti said she had to make her own way and work just as hard as everyone else before her.

In recent years brokerage firms have been encouraged by groups like NOW to hire more women. Patti said she is concerned with this type of hiring on gender rather than ability. She also resents being lumped into "the female group" instead of being recognized purely as the competent broker that she is.

Dr. Amy Coene Bales is the only female in her cardiology section. She said she is fortunate that her male co-workers have children and therefore have some understanding of her responsibilities as a mother in connection with her responsibilities as cardiologist. But these men have the privilege of being able to focus on their careers. Their wives are full-time homemakers. Their energies are not divided between family, home, and career as Amy's are. Working part-time, Amy said she cannot accomplish as much as the other doctors can. She said she often feels she is not doing a good enough job at home or at work. She has a sense of guilt that she is not pulling her weight.

Amy said sometimes she would like to focus on just one facet of her life. She would like to devote her time and concentration in one direction. Working in a male-dominated environment, Amy said few co-workers truly understand her struggle. Amy said underneath it all, women are women, and most have children. Having kids is in direct conflict with what should be done professionally. Any job, especially in a field with a lot of men, makes it hard to find that balance.

Anna Cheng Catalano, Senior Marketing Vice President of Sales Operations, began her career in the early 1980s at Amoco as a summer intern. She said she had many wonderful mentors at different times of her career, but being one of the first women to move through the ranks in the oil industry, a few of the other men were reluctant to mentor her. They feared the relationship would be thought to extend beyond the professional setting. There also were company parties where Amy said the men's wives made her feel uncomfortable.

Anna said she did not fight a lot of battles for equal rights during her career. She never experienced outright harassment, but there were situations that would be considered inappropriate today. Most of the time, when someone made a derogatory comment or gesture, she would bite her tongue. The few women who did not, developed a reputation of being difficult. As a result, Anna promised herself that if she got to a more strategic position where she could make a change, she would. Overall, Anna said Amoco did and still has a family atmosphere. Most of the time someone was willing to help. She said Amoco laid a good foundation for mentoring to occur from the very start.

Anna found understanding the male culture to be beneficial. Possessing a general knowledge of football, baseball, and golf allowed her to participate in conversations before Monday morning meetings. She said it helped that she actually enjoyed talking about sports.

But one of her greatest challenges in her career was handling her own overwhelming sense of responsibility to succeed. Anna said she never wanted to let down her gender. She had to really know her stuff. "Society is unforgiving to women at the top. It expects you to be everything to everyone, at home and at work. I had to learn to forgive myself for not being perfect," she said.

In the absence of senior women with whom to consult, Anna sought out those she could find in positions above and below her as well as outside the company. She joined networking groups and talked to other business women about what she calls common sense issues. Anna particularly missed having a woman mentor when she and her husband Joel decided to start a family. She had been married ten years. Anna was transferred to Omaha and then Milwaukee while Joel remained in Chicago. She had no one to talk to about a woman's corporate climb in the oil industry, a commuter marriage, and the integration of parenthood into such an intense career.

The solutions Anna and Joel found may be considered unconventional to mainstream America but have worked for the Catalanos. Anna was relocated to China for a year. Joel and their two children accompanied her. Joel took a leave from his structural engineering job and stayed home with the children. When they returned to the states, Joel worked part-time so he could be available for the children while Anna put in the extra hours needed at work and for business travel. Today, Joel is the full-time at-home parent.

The New Frontier

Few of us know someone in a similar situation to our own and who can totally mentor us in all facets of our professional or personal life. For some there is no one who can offer any guidance because our responsibilities are so different from anyone else's.

Several of The Fabulous Fifty-Two are in areas new or unusual to men and women alike. They have no one to go to for mentoring because no one has done exactly what they are doing. Finding a mentor becomes more challenging under these mutable conditions. For the most part, they had to find their own way, blaze their own trail entirely.

Dr. Helen Bonny had mentors for other parts of her life, but no one could have mentored her in the well-defined and developed content of GIM therapy, because she was its creator.

Linaya Hahn didn't intentionally set out to become an educator of Pre-Menstrual Syndrome. She delved into the study of PMS because she could not find answers to her own health concerns and was frustrated with her physical condition. No doctor offered her concrete answers or relief from her symptoms which continued to progress in intensity. Her life quest became the investigation of PMS, its symptoms, and solutions. Linaya said she was 35 years-old and wondering what she was going to be when she grew up. Then she got PMS and found out what she needed to do.

Few women were attorneys when Vicky Bush-Joseph entered the field. But Vicky went a step further by founding a practice with her two partners that is limited to adoption and infertility law. Adoption and infertility law and our ethical interpretation of new procedures is developing and modifying as technology offers us more and more complicated choices.

Vicky said other attorneys now call on her and her partner for answers to questions and for direction. Being the first to do what her practice does, Vicky feels obliged to mentor. If she did not, those attorneys would have no one else to go to for guidance on such complicated topics and the complicated law that goes with it. "It's a brave new world," said Vicky.

Dr. Ruth Martens decided she wanted to be a doctor when she was a child. She had fallen into some weeds and cut open her arm. She was fascinated watching her doctor stitch her wound and asked an endless list of questions. But on her pathway to becoming a doctor, Ruth became somewhat discouraged. She felt something was lacking in the way she wanted to practice medicine. A friend told her about homeopathy. She investigated further and saw homeopathy as the missing piece to her future medical practice. She would never had guessed earlier on her path to medicine that she would have to go to Greece to learn about the alternative practice because no expert could be found at that time in our country.

Eta-Lyn Lampert knows no one else who does exactly what she does. She never imagined she would grow up to be an executive assistant to an award-winning master magician. Her unusual path began after graduation from her New York high school. The honor-roll student and dancer surprised her family by joining the Ringling Brothers Circus. Dancing, riding elephants, and performing aerial stunts were exciting and an opportunity Eta-Lyn does not regret. However, she did regret leaving the circus five years later for a man.

Eta-Lyn took a job with the Internal Revenue Department. The contrast between the life in the circus to her new restrictive desk position was stifling. She said that time period was the worst time of her life.

Depressed, Eta-Lyn took a leave of absence. She went to Las Vegas to visit a friend from the circus and never went back. Eta-Lyn got a job dealing black jack in a casino during the day. She later took a night position as assistant to Magician Lance Burton. As Lance's career grew, so did Eta-Lyn's responsibilities, so she quit the casino job.

Lance performs two shows a night, five days a week at the Lance Burton Theater at the Monte Carlo Hotel in Las Vegas. Eta-Lyn said her responsibilities are varied, much like being a mom. She assists Lance with his show preparation and paper work. She acts as hostess for special guests escorted to Lance's personal reception room after shows. She oversees his checkbook and is certain he eats a healthy dinner. She even appears in a small part in his show.

Eta-Lyn said she would love to have had someone to mentor her in her assistant position. Occasionally, someone calls her for help. But Eta-Lyn said it is difficult to help another executive assistant, even in the entertainment field, because there are so many variances. Responsibilities and the approach to those responsibilities have to be customized to the entertainer and the particular show.

Overall, Eta-Lyn said she loves her unique position. She said working for Lance is a pleasure because he is considerate, professional, and extremely talented. "I believe in Lance Burton," said Eta-Lyn. "I absolutely love working for him."

Let your light so shine before men, that they may see your good works and glorify your Father in heaven.

Matthew
5:16

Chapter Eleven

BEING A LIGHTHOUSE

Rev. M. Sue Storm remembers attending a funeral for Dr. Carl List when she was a child. Dr. List was a highly respected neurosurgeon in her community. The funeral drew a tremendous turnout. Sue said the prevailing conversation was not only in recognition of the doctor's outstanding accomplishments but also about the tragic loss of his wealth of knowledge. Dr. List had never shared his insight and findings with another doctor. There would be no one to carry on his brilliant work, no one else to benefit from what he had learned. Sue said that funeral left an impact on her about the importance of passing on what we know to other people.

Imagine if no one ever passed on what they knew about anything to anyone else. What if we had to learn everything for ourselves? What if parents, teachers, and supervisors did not prepare, inform, or train us? How could any of us go beyond the knowledge and experiences of a caveman if each of us had to discover fire and invent the wheel?

Like lighthouses, mentors shed light on paths that we may not otherwise see. They give us a glimpse of where they have been so that we may learn from their experiences. Those of The Fabulous Fifty-Two who have been blessed with a mentor recognize the significance that person had on their entire life. They feel obligated to do the same for someone else, obligated to pass on the gift of mentoring.

AMA President Dr. Nancy W. Dickey said she is pleased and daunted by the number of women medical students who come into her office to question her about her career. These students are not necessarily interested in duplicating Nancy's path, but they hope to apply a variation of what they learn from her to their own career. Being the first woman to have been elected president of the AMA, Nancy said it is her responsibility to help others realize all possibilities are open to them also.

Nancy said everybody needs someone to reassure them that they can end up at the top. Having a mentor is reassuring, especially when breaking new ground. You may not choose the same pathway as your mentor, but you will be able to see a pathway through the mountains.

Susan Schreter, president of Caring Products International, said women regularly come to her looking for guidance on establishing their own business. They have not had the exposure to the business world that Susan feels she was privileged to have had since she was a child. She feels it is her duty to share what she knows and who she knows with other women who have not experienced such opportunity.

Leslie Wheeler Hortum, the senior vice-president at the U. S. Chamber of Commerce, said she gained so much from her mentors. She enjoys the bonds she feels with those who have helped her. She said when she mentors other people she is extending the gift her mentors shared with her.

Not sharing information is like having a precious jewel and sealing it in a vault where no one can enjoy its beauty, preparing a gourmet meal and not allowing anyone to savor the delicacies, or creating a moving concerto only to silence it away in the piano bench. Information has no value if no one knows it exists or is touched by it.

Dr. Monique Anawis, eye surgeon, said that mentoring gives value to what she has learned. Someone believed the knowledge they had was important enough to share it with her. Monique then does the same, passing this precious information on to someone else who will use it, grow from it, and help someone heal because of it.

Monique said she must take time to mentor medical students, friends, co-workers and patients. She has been fortunate to meet many people who have coached and mentored her. Since they took the time to pass on what they know to her, she said she must continue to move that information down the line to the next interested party.

Dr. Ruth Martens said she shares her knowledge of homeopathy with others eager to learn for two reasons. One is that she believes in homeopathy's tremendous ability to heal. Secondly, she wants to offer others the opportunity to learn the healing art without going to the extent she did to learn it. Ruth's extensive knowledge of homeopathy is an unusual commodity in this country. Here we have very limited resources of information on this method of treating disease. Ruth has taken several trips to Greece to study homeopathy at a great personal financial burden. She extends its benefits by incorporating it into her medical practice and teaching people in our country how to use it safely and effectively.

Ruby Frank, founder and president of Frank's Employment, said she sees mentoring as part of her job responsibilities. She understands the job market and relationship between employers and potential employees. She listens to candidates' concerns, evaluates their skills, and advises them on steps to consider in order to advance their career. Ruby creates win/win situations between employers and potential employees by sending well-prepared candidates to fill their perfect niche in the job market. Without the extra mentoring, placement would not be as successful.

Many people approach Harriet Gerber Lewis, chairman of the board of Gerber Plumbing Fixtures, Corp., to request her to mentor them. She is highly respected in the plumbing fixture industry, as well as the Jewish community, philanthropic organizations, and her family for her strength, courage, knowledge, experience, and generosity.

Sharing what she knows and what she has is what makes "Harriet" Harriet. Her grandson was recently quoted in Craines Chicago Business magazine as saying his grandmother taught him everything he knew about business. Her son calls her "menschmaker" - a Jewish term for someone who is good and gentle. Harriet said she is most proud of the times in her life when she reached out to help other people because that was when she was doing what we are all meant to do.

Anna Cheng Catalano, senior marketing vice president of sales operations for BP Amoco Petroleum Products, said she finds herself mentoring more and more often. She said when someone seeks her help she cannot say no, because she would have given anything for someone to help her when she was moving up the ranks at Amoco.

Anna said that in the past, survival was difficult for women at Amoco. It was not unusual for a woman to be divorced two or three times while employed there. They had to sacrifice their personal life if they wished to succeed in their career. The time invested in getting ahead at Amoco put a strain on even the best marriages.

Today that scenario is changing. Amoco women gather to discuss the obstacles they are encountering and share their solutions on how those obstacles can be avoided. They are taking more personal interest in assisting each other to advance their careers.

"We (women) have to be best friends," Anna said. "It's important for us to never forget to turn around and give a hand to the next in line as we climb that ladder. There is plenty of room at the top for outstanding performers. We owe it to each other to assist one another with that climb."

Behavior of a Mentor

Successful people function under a spotlight. We look to them as role models and mentors, because we want to learn how we can be successful too. Judy Chaffee, professional training consultant for Chrysler Corporation and public speaker, said mentors need to be aware of the audience they draw and act accordingly. Mentors must walk the talk and demonstrate the proper behavior they are teaching the protégé.

Dr. Nancy Dickey said mentoring comes with significant responsibility. The best mentors know others are watching what, and how, they are doing. She said these mentors are more aware of their shortcomings. They control their temper, insensitivity to other people's feelings, and self-serving goals and aspirations.

Alice Umbach, psychotherapist, said giving advice is easy, but the mentor must also live what is taught. She said productive mentoring is sharing what you have been through, and not complaining about it, but using those experiences to become a better person. It is showing the next person that if you could do it, they could too.

Counselors Who Mentor

Counseling is a prime medium for mentoring. By attending visits with a counselor, clients are acknowledging the fact that they require assistance with development in a particular area. They seek a counselor who they trust will offer good direction. And hopefully, the client will follow the counselor's direction and remove barriers that obstruct personal growth.

Alice said she considers a therapist she saw a number of years ago as a mentor. Now she mentors many of the clients who come to her. Mentoring is a major part of her practice, particularly when working with women. Not everyone comes to her in crisis. Many just want to change their course. Alice expands their world, strives to raise their confidence, and pushes them to higher levels.

Kathy Ballman, high school and domestic violence counselor, said students come to her to discuss relationships they have with peers and parents. They also discuss their career and life plans. Students want to know what happens beyond high school. They are concerned about the steps they need to take to get to their future goals.

Kathy reaches out to students by sharing the factual information they need to know. She names people and organizations that could be of help to them. She shares what she has learned from her own personal experiences.

Rev. M. Sue Storm said as a mentor and metaphysical counselor she believes she must be available to her clients/protégés as much as possible. Sue can be reached by pager, car phone, and voice mail. She responds quickly to all calls. Sue said sometimes clients believe they are in a state of emergency. If she responds quickly, the clients' situation, or perception of their situation, can be relieved before it wears their physical or emotional state any further.

Sue said she sows seeds that rapidly develop in her clients/protégés. When someone has the intent to make progress in their life, the energy follows that intention. The ball starts rolling with the thought. Sue said it doesn't really have anything to do with her other than offering suggestions to the client as to how to get that ball moving.

Recipe for Mentoring

Although there are extensive variations of mentoring styles and ingredients among The Fabulous Fifty-Two, several indicated elements they believed important to the success of the mentor-protégé relationship. Dr. Cheryl Conover, Professor of Medicine at Mayo Clinic, said mentoring can't be mandated. A protégé must have respect for the mentor previously to working with that person. Also, there must be some chemistry between protégé and mentor. She said the chance for interaction increases when the mentor is someone you admire, but something still has to click between the two people.

Patti Doyle Brewer, stockbroker, said she believes mentoring works best when respect and admiration is mutual between protégé and mentor. The protégé must have those feelings for the mentor. The mentor is chosen because the protégé thinks the mentor is good at what she does. She wants to pick your brain and learn what you do and how you do it. The protégé hopes you will take them under your wing and learn from you face-to-face.

But Patti said that is only half the quotient. The protégé has to have the capacity and desire to learn. And the mentor has to identify that capacity and want to invest their time and knowledge into the other person.

As stated earlier, each of our circumstances is different not only from one another, but also from each of our own experiences. So the mentoring we need must be customized to each situation. Mentors have their own mentoring style that corresponds with their personality. Having the best mentor means matching the style and wisdom of a mentor with the situation on hand and the personality of the protégé.

Judy Chaffee is a veteran mentor. She said mentoring has been a fundamental element of her work for more than fifteen years. As a past college teacher, customer service representative, business owner, and a current corporate trainer, Judy has encountered many people who sought to learn from her. They want to know how she was able to accomplish what she has in business. She is asked to share her gifts, talents, experience, and time.

Judy enjoys mentoring and has found that it works best when it is "free flowing." The mentor recognizes where the protégé needs to improve, has the knowledge and ability to bring the protégé up to par, and holds the protégé's respect. This is all done in a casual as-needed basis. Judy said that's when you see outstanding results.

Marcia Balestri, geochemist, said she mentors other employees in an informal way because she is an informal type of person. When she notices someone in need of direction she gives that employee examples of her own past experiences in similar situations. She also projects scenarios of what they may encounter and then questions them as to how they would respond.

Kathleen Freeland, horticulturist, is surprised how often she hears other people in her field name her as their mentor. It is not unusual for employees to state in their exit interview from Midwest Groundcovers that Kathleen was more than a boss to them. She also was a mentor. She said she is not a structured person so her mentoring is also fluid and unstructured. She said she is very proud of that mentoring part of her, because it is absolutely critical in management and seems to happen without her actually trying.

Leslie Wheeler Hortum said she tries to mentor as much as possible. She mentors junior and senior high school students in the Operation Enterprise Youth Program that gives students a glimpse of the business world. She also mentors other U.S. Chamber of Commerce employees who she feels have potential to advance.

Leslie said she models her mentoring after her own experiences with mentors. She sets meetings with protégés to evaluate their progress. She offers opportunities to participate in a variety of projects and encourages them to jump in with both feet. Leslie said she gives protégés occasions to be a part of things and rise to the occasion.

Emily Emmerman, Vice President of Strategic Services at University of Chicago Hospitals, mentors several protégés. Her style is more formal. She develops specific goal plans. She sets monthly meetings with protégés to discuss strengths, weaknesses, and progress.

Susan Coe Heitsch, Vice President of Corporate Affairs at Bank One, takes on protégés as employees come under her wing as a manager. Her aggressive approach to mentoring includes scheduled meetings, evaluations, informal testing, goal plans, field trips to vendors, practice interviews, social opportunities to network with other employees and managers, and even recommended reading lists. Susan also gives protégés opportunity to prepare and present material at company meetings.

Marlene Tighe, retired area operations manager for Ameritech, said her mentoring style changed from when she started her career with Ohio Bell in 1956 until her recent retirement. Marlene's first professional mentors were mostly autocratic. One woman from whom she said she learned the business recited what to do by the book. She, like most of the early bosses, was more technical rather than managerial.

About thirty years later, Judy Chaffee was brought in by the company to teach a program called "Impression Management." The program was to improve oral and visual communication at all levels of the company. Every employee was included in the program from management down through craft, customer service, billing, and collections. Self-directed teams, the necessity of assuming responsibility, self-motivation, and striving for one's personal best was encouraged in this program.

Initially, Marlene resisted the new training. She said she thought it would be like going to charm school. She couldn't believe employees could be trained to take on responsibility. "That would be like allowing the inmates to do the work," Marlene said.

But to her surprise, the first attendants claimed the program to be unbelievable. They were gushing with enthusiasm. After Marlene met Judy, she was convinced of the program's benefits and went back to her boss and told him to take it to the front line.

Marlene said her management style changed because of the program and Judy's direction. She found the biggest transformation in developing self-directed teams to happen in the manager. Therefore, she couldn't be a traditional manager anymore after teaching others how to be self-directed. She had to let go of the old style and take on the role of coach and mentor. She said she had to pay attention to the human side and nurture champions.

The Cost of Mentoring

Kahil Gibran writes about the parent-child relationship in his book, *The Prophet*. Gibran uses the metaphor of a bow and arrow to describe the parent-child relationship saying parents are the bows and children are the arrows. It is the parent's responsibility to send the child out into the world like the bow projects the arrow. He also said parents can give children their love but not their thoughts. Children have their own thoughts.

Gibran's words can be applied to mentoring. The mentor's job is to send the protégé out better prepared and able to succeed. A mentor can pass on knowledge, but the protégé's thoughts and actions resulting from this knowledge belong to them. The protégés' future and successes also belong to them.

Alice Umbach said the challenge in mentoring and counseling is in keeping the ego out of the relationship. If you have it in your mind that a client needs to do something or take a particular course, and then they don't follow your advice, you can't get upset. Nor can you take credit for the work they do. You are there for support.

When I was gathering research for this book, I asked a number of women who do not mentor, why they do not. The answers were as varied as the women and their complicated lives. Many said they do not have the time to mentor. Although Anna Cheng Catalano does mentor, she said her greatest price for mentoring is finding the time to do it. After hours required for work and family, little is left to offer someone else. She said taking all that personal time to mentor is draining. It has to be done before or after work or on weekends.

Other women said they did not mentor because they didn't feel they had anything to offer. They did not recognize any unusual talent or ability in themselves important enough to pass on to someone else.

A few women actually said they liked knowing what they, and no one else, knew. That knowledge made them feel important and special. They liked owning a powerful edge over everyone else.

Mentoring requires generosity. When we mentor, we give someone else something that will allow their life to become easier because of our hard work in the past. Since knowledge is power, mentoring - the sharing of knowledge and wisdom - is empowering. It takes confidence to share power with someone who may go further in life than we have with what we give them.

Emily Emmerman said mentoring puts the mentor in a vulnerable position. The mentor's reputation is on the line. She said promoting and pushing someone is risky. They are not always successful, and you are held accountable.

Sandy Oler, Bible study leader and church volunteer, said one challenge she experienced in mentoring was being able to let go of responsibilities that she was proud of handling. About ten years ago Sandy was selling office furniture. She was expecting her first child and needed to hire someone to take over her accounts. Sandy said the outcome of her training and mentoring was professionally successful, but personally difficult. She felt like she was handing over her children.

Judy Chaffee said mentoring takes patience and the courage to stand back and allow the protégé to take center stage. She said, "as mentors we shine other people's stars. We are not the stars."

The Rewards of Mentoring

Like everything that has a price, mentoring also has rewards. Diana Dionisio-Pieczynski, manager of publicity and promotions at WGN-TV, said the station often hires interns. She needs the physical assistance of the interns as much as they need to learn from her experience. The true reward of the relationship is seeing the interns come in with limited experience and walk away with added professionalism and self-confidence. Overall, Diana said she enjoys building the interns.

Emily Emmerman agreed with Diana. She said the return of mentoring is in witnessing the creativity of the protégé and the satisfaction in her protégés' growth. Emily said when someone is bright and enthusiastic, it is exciting to participate in their development.

Sue Storm added that her goal is to aide clients in the advancement of their personal growth. That's what her career is all about. She feels good when good things happen to other people. She enjoys seeing a light in their eyes or hearing it in their voice.

Several of The Fabulous Fifty-Two said they learn more about the topic they are working on with their protégés and also about many life issues from their experiences with mentoring. Allison Barnett said when she teaches T'ai Chi Ch'uan for Barnett Martial Arts, she is emotionally moved by students older than her who approach her for direction. Through teaching she is learning how to be a better communicator and instructor, and she is learning more about T'ai Chi. Allison said you can't really know something until you teach it.

Judy Chaffee said mentoring promotes individual growth. You find out who you are and what you can handle through mentoring. In the end she finds the results very gratifying.

Fabulous Fifty-Two Models of Mentoring

The Fabulous Fifty-Two recount particular occasions of mentoring which have touched their lives as much as their protégés. Janet Faye Damm mentored an employee at Ford Motor Credit Company where she works as a credit analyst. She helped the employee with her responsibilities as well as her presentation to upper management. She encouraged her to return to school for additional credentials. Janet prompted her to ask for a raise and promotion, which the employee did receive and received significantly earlier than she would have without Janet's prompting.

Debbie McElroy, registered nurse, said she mentored a friend who became a widow at the age of 27 years old. The young woman also was a nurse before she had her children. Debbie guided her friend in exploring her options, sharpening her skills, and returning to the work force. Debbie said she helped her friend make that leap from mommy to working person.

The mentoring experience between Ruth Chodak, Vice President of Business Development at University of Chicago Hospitals and Health System, and Emily Emmerman was significant to both of them. Ruth has mentored many of her employees. The learning, growth, and bond formed between Ruth and Emily was much more intense than any other experience either had encountered.

Ruth said when she called Emily into her office for an interview, she was not hiring at the time. She remembered hearing Emily's name from a recruiter some months previously and was curious. She had not anticipated the outcome that would transpire from that initial meeting.

Ruth said she knew immediately when she met Emily that she was somebody who could grow into the job. "She had that spark. Emily could take my place someday. Some people you have to drag along. I knew this woman would be easy. Emily had a lot of drive and ambition. She was just a slight little thing, very petite. She didn't have a lot on her resume, yet she exuded confidence, which was interesting to see in someone her age," said Ruth.

Ruth called another vice president into her office to meet

Emily. Then Ruth and the vice president stepped out of the room. The vice president said to Ruth that he thought she met her match. Ruth admits to a moment of intimidation by that statement. She said she thought Emily could exceed her own potential. But she immediately caught herself and decided to do whatever she could to mentor Emily.

Ruth identified Emily's strengths and weaknesses. She said Emily was lacking what she calls a bag of tricks, tools and skills that are acquired through experience. She lacked business discipline and advanced education. However, Emily was a great observer. She learned quickly by watching other people and emulating them. Ruth said Emily could take feedback with dignity and not get blown away.

Ruth gave Emily opportunity to learn and grow. Gradually Emily began taking over more and more meetings. Afterwards Ruth evaluated and discussed situation after situation with Emily pointing out where and how she could improve. Ruth said some of her challenges in mentoring Emily included allowing Emily to make mistakes, knowing when to offer assistance and when to remain silent, letting Emily work through situations on her own, and keeping her own ego out of the relationship.

When Emily took over Ruth's old job, Ruth said she had handed over her baby. Emily had big shoes to fill. Ruth had to step back and let her shine. Most importantly, she had to let Emily know she trusted her and had confidence in her. Ruth said their relationship has often felt much like that powerful exchange between a parent and child. She had to remind herself the greatest compliment to her would be to have Emily do well after her mentoring.

Ruth typically does not get too friendly with employees. But she said she enjoys a more personal relationship with Emily today since they are no longer superior and subordinate. Now they can be friends and peers. Ruth said their friendship is very special.

Emily said she truly appreciates all that Ruth has done for her. She is grateful for the opportunities that have been presented to her because of Ruth and continues the gift of mentoring in her honor. "When somebody has that much impact on you, how can you not pass that along?" Emily said.

Chapter Twelve

CALLING YOU TO MENTOR

An employee at Ford Motor Credit Company told Janet Faye Damm, Credit Analyst, that the key to forward movement in the company for a man is to have a happy home life. But for a woman the key is not to have a family.

Janet said she disagrees with that assessment. The way to attain success cannot be generalized. She believes there never is a clear, straight path to the top. There are so many differences and variations. If she was asked to relocate again, she certainly would have to consider her husband Tom's career and her sons' welfare. But Janet said Tom offers as much support for her career growth as she does for him. The decision would be based on their situation as a family at that time.

Dr. Jeannette Martens Sorrentino's parents always were supportive of her dental training and career, but she remembers once in graduate school her brother asked her why she was working so hard. She would only be getting married and having children some day. Now that she is married with three daughters, she sees her struggle to balance her roles as dentist, wife, and mother even more important. She says she wants to be a positive example to her daughters of how to blend profession and family life.

In a previous chapter Dr. Cheryl Conover made a statement about the importance of having support at home and at work. Sometimes that daily network of support needs to be fairly extensive to truly maintain a sense of balance. Being able to delegate responsibilities we do not wish to do, we do not do best, or are unable to do, allows us to have more time and energy for what we do best.

My daughter, Lisa, recently told me she looks forward to the day she can hire a housekeeper. She said housekeeping is not something she enjoys or does well. She'd prefer to work overtime on her job. She could earn more money than it would cost for the service.

Lisa's remark makes me a bit uncomfortable because I've been raised to believe housework is my responsibility even if I work full time and had a family to care for. However, I am changing my train of thought. Today I do have a housekeeper. Peggy is a wonderful woman who scrubs our house from top to bottom twice a month. Peggy is conscientious, efficient, and cheerful. She has become a trusted friend as well as a valued employee. Not only am I learning to accept her help, I'm finding I would like her here more often. Life is so much easier when I don't play the martyr and frantically try to cover all the bases.

BP Amoco Senior Vice President Anna Cheng Catalano reminds her protégés that they have 100% energy to give. That 100% can only be divided in so many ways. How they wish to spend that energy is a choice worth considering before hitting a point of frustration and exhaustion.

The Honorable Hollis Webster has a live-in au pair to assist with child-care and housekeeping. She said her husband and extended family members also are supportive. She attributes her success in balancing everything to the extent of people helping her. Hollis said we are kidding ourselves if we believe we can do everything ourselves.

Leslie Wheeler Hortum, Senior Vice President for Federation Development for the U. S. Chamber of Commerce, has a substantial network of support to assist with the care of her two young children and home. She employs Maureen Patton, a full-time-live-in nanny. Her husband, Episcopal Priest J.D. (John), prepares meals and shops for the groceries. Leslie's mother and mother-in-law eagerly fill in as needed.

Leslie said she can't underemphasize the support she has. She couldn't work the hours she does without them. The level of child care they provide makes all the difference to her. Because of her support team she can go out the door in the morning with ease of mind.

Cardiologist Dr. Amy Coene Bales has a nanny at home and a nurse at the office to help her out. She said she couldn't do her job without either one of them. Amy understands her own strengths and needs and calls on the resources available to her to assist with the responsibilities she can delegate.

Cheryl Conover said in addition to her husband's support, she balances her tremendous responsibilities at the Mayo Clinic with those in her personal life by limiting the hours she spends in the office. She calls herself the "Cinderella Scientist." Cheryl said she does not stay late or work weekends. She said something is wrong if she's still at work after 5:00 PM.

Not everyone can limit those hours at work. With all the help possible, many people still find the days too short to complete everything that has to be done. Emily Emmerman, Vice President and Corporate Officer at Louis A. Weiss Memorial Hospital, University of Chicago, said she finds juggling personal and professional responsibilities to be challenging.

In her position, attendance at late night work meetings is vital to acquiring necessary information. She is a wife and mother with family obligations and considerations. She enjoys visits with family and friends and feels that time is important to maintain those relationships. Emily also manages stress and cares for her physical and mental health with sessions at the health club. And of course, she always has a lengthy list of household chores to complete. Emily said after all these obligations, she finds that list of chores to be the easiest to delegate to someone else, but that still leaves little time for herself. She said at the end of the day, she remains the loser.

Even with Leslie Wheeler Hortum's extensive support system, she also said sometimes she feels personally shortchanged. She rarely gets enough sleep and would like to have more contact with other women friends.

Linaya Hahn, PMS Educator, suggests putting ourselves on our "to do" list. Blocking out time on our calendar to walk in the park or just sit in a hot bathtub with a good book will benefit ourselves, and ultimately, everyone else in our life because we will feel happier and more rested.

Dr. Ruth Martens' escape takes her a little further than her bathtub. She is an airplane pilot and enjoys the beauty and challenge of flying above the clouds. She says those solitary flights are both relaxing and invigorating for her and a wonderful diversion from her medical practice. Ruth said she enjoys the fact that no one can reach her in the sky.

One of the first college courses I took when I returned to school was a speech class. The first day each student told about themselves, the many committees to which they belonged, and the activities in which they were involved. About half way around the room, a woman from Atlanta said in her lovely, southern droll, "You all talk about what you do. What do I do? I sit - on the verandah. I sip - iced tea. That is what I do."

At first, the class laughed at the woman. But then after a few moments, we stopped, and laughed at ourselves. We had to ask ourselves why we don't take the time to sit on the verandah. Is whatever we are doing really so important?

High achievers don't relax well. If we watch television, we must also read a book. If we take our children to the playground, we bring paperwork along to complete while we sit on the park bench. If we have a long commute to work, we listen to books on tape or learn a language.

This marvelous world of ours has so much to offer. I don't want to miss a bit of it. But I also don't want to miss out on the glory of the moment. As much as I read, see, do, and meet other people, I also try to take some time to relish what is in front of me. I am striving to see the forest and the trees.

M-E-N-T-O-R Spells Success

In addition to a support system at home and at work, Susan Coe Heitsch, Vice President of Corporate Affairs at Bank One, pointed out a formula for achievement. She calls this formula the "ABCD's of Success." She said to succeed we need:

A - Ability
B - Breaks
C - Courage, and
D - Determination.

We must have the ability to do the job, the breaks or opportunity to use our ability, the courage to take the steps necessary to move forward, and the determination to get where we want to go against all odds for success to be the result.

And, as this book stresses, having someone behind you to support, direct, and accelerate your growth can make all the difference. The mentor can help to identify your abilities, offer the breaks, encourage the courage, and light the fire of determination.

Ruth Chodak, Vice President of Business Development for the University of Chicago Hospitals & Health System, said a leader will rise to the top eventually, with or without a mentor. But having a mentor is critical in reaching that point sooner. Those who have been blessed with a mentor have no doubt about their tremendous significance. The path to the top is clearer and quicker because of the mentor who reaches across the road to share their self with another person.

Anita Smith, music contractor, said that not only do mentors make a difference in another human being's life but all the lives that touch that person. She would not be the same person if she hadn't had her mother, Hilda, and old boss and friend, Henry, as mentors. Their influence is at least partly responsible for the way she relates to the other people around her.

Kathy Ballman, domestic violence and adolescent counselor, said mentors didn't change her course but are changing the rate in which she is moving within her career. They also have identified talents she did not recognize within herself. She said she is looking forward to the day when she can do that for someone else, when she can return what her mentors have done for her.

As the year of participation in the Mentoring for Leadership business program drew to a close for Laurie Scordo, owner of Laurel Gifts, Laurie reflected on the program's benefits. She said she knows she has grown because of the program and Cheryl, her mentor. She is grateful for the wonderful, positive experience. She said she has come such a long way this year. She has miles to go, but she looks forward with enthusiasm and hope that in the future she can offer the same kind of experience to anyone who might look to her for mentoring.

No Limits leader and artist, Debra Trent, said the peer mentoring relationships formed in the No Limits for Women Artists' seminars are vital to artists. She added that it doesn't matter what type of art they practice. Debra said there is something about being able to sit down with someone who shares your interests and excitement about the same career, even if the two of you aren't practicing the same medium.

Leslie Wheeler Hortum advises not to wait to be mentored but go out and find a mentor if you don't have one. We don't get anywhere alone, so don't be afraid to ask for help. Watch the people around you, and then approach someone from whom you'd like to learn. Invite the potential mentor to lunch. Tell them why you would like to work with them and what you would like to learn. If they refuse to mentor you, accept their decline gracefully. If they agree, remember to respect them and their personal space at all times. They are sharing the priceless gift of themselves.

Rev. M. Sue Storm recommends consulting more than one mentor if possible. She said different mentors offer different viewpoints and advice from which a protégé can draw in making a decision. We are all gifted in certain areas. So it's best to consult a variety of people to make a good decision. Sue said she knows she doesn't have all the answers. Her objective is to empower, not retain power. She asks clients how they feel about what she tells them and suggests that they not do what feels uncomfortable to them.

The Mentor in You

An article by Michelle Weldon in the March 1, 1998 issue of the *Chicago Tribune* stated that in a recent survey, African-American, Asian-American, and Hispanic women feel their advancement is inhibited by a lack of influential mentors and women of their ethnic background in high level positions in the workplace. More than 1,700 women were surveyed, and more than half of this group was middle management.

You are key to changing that scenario. Mentoring another woman in your business, whether you are a man or a woman, will help to raise that person, yourself, and everyone else in both of your lives. I recently read about a woman named Margaret Litterman who is retired and living in Kauai, Hawaii. Margaret worked as a school psychologist for 20 years. During her career, Margaret's husband, Stanley, told her to invest her income as she wished, and he would care for the family's financial needs. Margaret invested in school scholarships for children at the school where she worked and those in Kauai. She said she had everything she needed. She wanted to invest in people and the future of our global society rather than the stock market.

We are surrounded by opportunities to invest in others. We touch so many lives in our home, community, travels, and at work. After receiving her Bachelor of Arts Degree in Business Administration and Management, my daughter Lisa was hired by Carole M. Rogin, President of Clarion Management Resources, Inc. in Alexandria, Virginia. Clarion offers everything from telephone answering, clerical, functional, and administrative services to financial management as well as the production and distribution of direct mailings and promotional materials on a contract basis. Organizations which could not afford the daily services of a full staff commission Clarion to do the work as needed.

Lisa said Carole considers mentoring her employees to be a priority in her business. Carol hires employees in which she identifies potential to excel and exceed the training and guidance she intends to provide. She is generous with encouragement, compliments, and concrete advice. Lisa said Carol made her feel important, that she was worth something to the company.

Lisa has since moved back to Illinois. She works for Air Angels, an emergency transport company, and once again, is being mentored by a supervisor, Michael Dermont. Lisa has become quite confident in giving presentations to hospital and fire department staffs as a result of Mike's coaching.

Employers like Carole and Mike often see their employees grow and outgrow their business, leaving for higher level positions elsewhere. But the alternative to developing your employees and seeing them leave is that they don't develop and stay with your company as a stagnant member of your team. When we mentor, we gain a better employee for the remainder of their employment with our company. We also gain information through our teaching and their learning, their respect, and their friendship.

Career Links Director Linda Shepard said mentoring offers a new perspective when we look at situations through the eyes of a protégé. Connecting with young women in Career Links helps Linda look at the world with the young protégé's sense of wonder and hope. "Sometimes I have to ask myself when I started being my mother, when did I stop believing in possibilities? The young women who come here renew the hope in me with their blind faith," Linda said.

Judy Chaffee said successful leaders surround themselves with people who are far better than themselves.

We grow when we promote growth in others.

Carol Havey, author of *Women and Self-Confidence*, reminds us that everyone has something to offer as a mentor. Our experiences are all unique. And we are never too old to mentor. Remember, Carol said her best mentor is her 100 year old mother.

We have a saying in writing, "Show, not tell." Nurse Debbie McElroy said that storytelling is an important part of mentoring. She doesn't want to hear all the technical garbage. She wants to know the truth and feel the reality of it all. Storytelling passes on our faith, knowledge, and history in a way in which we can visualize and grasp on an emotional level.

This book, *MENTORING HEROES*, is based on that principal. It's really another form of mentoring. Rather than outlining everything you might do to find a mentor, to be mentored, and to mentor, I pass on the stories on behalf of The Fabulous Fifty-Two so that you may learn and grow from the stories of their experiences and their wisdom.

I end this book with a request to you to be a leader, up close and personal. I invite you to invest a part of yourself into a future hero. Reach out and share your gifts with someone, so they may pass on what they gain from you to their protégés. By you helping me, me helping the next person, and that person helping another, together we can make our world a better, brighter place.

APPENDIX

APPENDIX

THE FABULOUS FIFTY-TWO

Anawis, M.D., Monique is an eye physician, surgeon, and Director of Ophthalmology Teaching for University of Chicago Hospitals. She has two offices in Chicago, Illinois and one in the suburb of Lake Bluff. She received her Medical Degree, Bachelor of Arts in Biology, and Bachelor of Arts in Anthropology from Brown University. Monique is fluent in Polish. She was a competitive ice skater from the age of eight years old through her high school years.

Balestri, Marcia E. is a geochemist and the Vice President and Director of the Environmental Technology Development Group at TRW, Inc. She received her Masters of Science degree in Geology from the University of New Mexico in 1979, her Bachelor of Arts degrees in Geology and Chemistry from the University of North Carolina in 1975. Marcia's awards include the American Metals Climax Corporation Scholarship, and the Grant-in-Aid from the New Mexico Geological Society. She is affiliated with the American Chemical Society and Sigma Xi. Marcia is fluent in Spanish. She resides in Frederick, Maryland with her husband, Robert Balestri. *Please note*: since completion of this book, Marcia has left her position at TRW and started her own company, Avalon Conusuting Group, Inc. She has acquired two prime contracts with the Department of Energy and two subcontracts with two other companies, one of which is TRW.

Ballman, Kathy is a counselor at a domestic violence shelter and Lancaster High School. She is attending Prescott College for a Masters Degree. Kathy resides in Lancaster, California with her husband, Mark Ballman, and their 18 year-old son.

Barnett, Allison is the owner, graphic artist, and illustrator for Moonwolf Graphics+. She also teaches T'ai Chi Ch'uan for Barnett Martial Arts. Allison graduated from California State University-San Bernadino with a Bachelor of Arts degree in English. She was honored in high school with a scholarship to Art Center College of Design in Pasedena that she attended for two years. She has published her first book on poetry, *The Song of Enchantment,* under the pen name Allison Deputy. Allison is married to Herb Barnett and lives in South Elgin, Illinois. She is 33 years old.

Bonny, Ph.D., R.M.T., Helen L. is an international teacher, public speaker, author, and violinist. She is the co-founder and director of The Bonny Foundation, a non-profit institute for music-centered therapies. She developed Guided Imagery and Music (GIM), an holistic form of transformational therapy which incorporates psychology, music, and spirituality. Helen taught at The Catholic University of America in Washington, DC and was a member of the clinical staff at the Maryland Psychiatric Research Center during the 1970s. She is the author *of Music and Your Mind* in addition to several other books and articles. She is concertmaster of the Salina Symphony Orchestra and a violin instructor. Helen received a Ph.D. from Union Institute in 1976 and a Bachelor Degree in music from Oberlin Conservatory of Music in 1943. Helen has three grown children to whom she refers as her "jewels." They are Beatrice Stoner, Erich Lind Bonny, and Francis Albert Bonny. She also has seven grandchildren. Helen is 77 years old.

Brewer, Patti (Patricia) Doyle is Second Vice-President for Solomon Smith Barney. She is a member of the Bond Club of Chicago. She received a Bachelor of Arts degree from the University of Illinois at Chicago. Patti regularly volunteers at her daughter's school. She lives in Oak Park, Illinois with her husband, Parke Brewer, and eight year old daughter, Michelle. Patti was born on May 31, 1956.

Bush-Joseph, J.D., Vicky (Victoria) is an attorney and partner in the firm Bush-Joseph & Horwich in Chicago, Illinois, a practice limited to adoption and infertility law. Vicky served on the Board of Directors of RESOLVE of Illinois, the state chapter of the national organization, as its Director of Advocacy for more than seven years. She co-drafted the Illinois Family Building Act and co-directed RESOLVE's lobbying campaign to pass the law, which requires insurance coverage of medical treatment of infertility. She frequently speaks at events sponsored by RESOLVE and other entities on insurance coverage for infertility, the legalities of adoption, and other infertility related topics. Vicky received her law degree from Loyola

University in 1982 where she was a member of the Law Review and the Moot Court team. She graduated summa cum laude from Loyola University of Chicago in 1978. Vicky is a member of the American Academy of Adoption Attorneys, the Illinois State Bar Association, and the Chicago Bar Association. She is married and has three children ages seven, six, and two. Vicky is 42 years old.

Chaffee, Judy is a professional training consultant and public speaker. She developed and implemented customer-focused training with market-based strategies for the service industry. Key training topics include enhanced team dynamics with self-managed/high performance team concepts. Judy managed and directed the performance of an instructional training team for Chrysler Corporation's "Customer One" initiative involving more than 2,000 dealership personnel. Other clients include Ameritech, Amoco Oil, Baxter Healthcare Corporation, B.F. Goodrich, Kellogg Company, and McDonalds Corporation. Judy received a Master of Science degree from Southern Illinois University graduating Magnum Cum Loude. She received her Bachelor of Science degree also from Southern Illinois University. Judy is single. She has two children; Michael, 24 years old and Cathleen, 21 years old. Judy lives in Naperville, Illinois and is 51 years old.

Cheng Catalano, Anna is Senior Marketing Vice President of Sales Operations for BP Amoco Petroleum Products. She is responsible for managing and directing Amoco Petroleum Products' 34-state sales and operations organization. Previously, she served as Amoco's Chicago region marketing as Vice-President of International Business Development, Manager of Business Development in

China, Manager of Products Research, and various other positions including field sales, product pricing, strategic planning, total quality management, and national merchandising. She attended the Indiana University Executive Management Program in 1990 and received a Bachelor of Science Degree in Marketing and Business Administration from the University of Illinois in 1982. She is a board member of the Children's Miracle network telethon and the Junior Achievement Dupage County, Illinois and a nominating committee member for the Girl Scouts of America. Anna is a native of Kansas City, Missouri. She is married to Joel Catalano and currently lives in England. They have two children, daughter, Carson, and son, David. She is fluent in Mandarin Chinese. Her date of birth is September 3, 1959.

Chodak, Ruth A. is the vice president of business development for the University of Chicago Hospitals & Health System. Her education includes a Master of Business Administration degree from the University of Chicago, Graduate School of Business, Master of Arts in Counseling and Rehabilitation from New York University, and a Bachelor of Speech, Education of the Deaf from Northwestern University. Her past and present directorships and awards include Board of Directors for the Heartland Alliance, President of the Board of Directors for the Florence Heller Jewish Community Center, Secretary of the Uptown Chamber of Commerce, Kohl Children's Museum board member, Athena Award Recipient for Outstanding Business Women of the Year, Certificate with Highest Honors in the Computer Career Program at DePaul University, England Rotary International Fellowship Award for special education from the Lady Spencer Churchill College in Oxford, England, The Dean's List at the University of

Chicago, Beta Gamma Sigma Honorary Fraternity, full government scholarship to New York University, and full senior year scholarship to Northwestern University. Ruth is 44 years old. She has one son, David, born in 1989.

Coe Heitsch, Susan is the Vice President of Corporate Affairs at Bank One. She has been honored with the Leadership Award for Excellence in Management 1997, the Chicago Financial Advertiser's Award for "First Class" print advertising campaign, and the Trust Department's Distinguished Service Award. Susan received her Master of Management Degree in Finance and Marketing from Northwestern University in 1984 (Dean's List) and a Bachelor of Science in Marketing from DePaul University in 1980 (Summa Cum Laude). She was Named Outstanding Commerce Graduate of 1980. Other educational accomplishments include postgraduate studies in Emerging Payment Technologies, Communications Strategy, and New Product Development. Susan is a member of the American Marketing Association, Chicago Association of Direct Marketing, and the International Association of Business Communicators. She is married to Gary Heitsch. They have a four year old daughter, Kristin, and live in Palatine, Illinois.

Coene Bales, M.D., **Amy** is a cardiologist with the University of Chicago Hospitals and resides in Munster, Indiana. She received her medical degree from Cornell University Medical College, New York, New York in 1990 and her Bachelor of Science degree (with distinction) also from Cornell in 1986. Her honors and awards include the Leon Resenekov Award for Excellence in Clinical Cardiology, the John Metcalf Polk Prize for General Efficiency, the Janet

M. Glasgow Memorial Achievement Citation, and the Alpha Omega Alpha Honor Society. She is a member of the American College of Cardiology and the American Society of Echocardiography. Amy is married to Gregory Thomas Bales, M.D. and has a one year old daughter named Cayla. Amy's date of birth is September 1, 1964.

Conover, Ph.D., Cheryl is Professor of Medicine, Director of the Endocrine Research Unit, and Vice Chair for Research in the Department of Medicine at the Mayo Clinic in Minnesota. She is married to Jack Thomas and has three children: Jill, 13 years old, Stephanie, 11 years old, and Scott, 7 years old. Cheryl is 46 years old.

Cotterill, Margaret is a traffic manager for Cobra Electronics Corporation in Chicago, Illinois. She attended the University of Illinois at Chicago after high school and is currently resuming her undergraduate education. Margaret is married to James Cotterill and has two daughters, Kelly, seven years old, and Megan, five years old. They live in Lombard, Illinois. Margaret's birth date is January 10, 1962.

Damm, Janet Faye is a credit analyst for Ford Motor Credit Company. She served in the U.S. Navy from 1988 to 1992 as a Yeoman, E-4 with top secret clearance. She received a Bachelor of Science Degree in Finance from Northern Illinois University and an Associate in Art Degree in Business from Rock Valley College. Janet is married to Tom Damm and has two young sons: Nicholas and Ryan. Janet and her family live in Carrollton, Texas.

Darby, Sue (Susan) is First Vice President of Solomon Smith Barney, Inc. She has been a stockbroker for 36 years. Sue majored in English and has a bachelor degree from the University of Wisconsin-Madison. The Children's Home and Aide Society is one of the several boards on which she has served. Her husband, Edwin, is a journalist. They have one son, G.K. Darby. Sue lives in Chicago, Illinois.

Dimiceli-Mitran, M.T.-B.C., Louise is a musical performer, songwriter, producer of commercial music for Mitran Mitran Music, and board certified music therapist. She received her Music Therapist-Board Certified degree from Alverno College and Bachelor of Music Education degree from Drake University. She completed her music therapy internship at Lutheran General Hospital. Currently in private practice, Louise is affiliated with Strong Spirit Wellness Center at Illinois Masonic Hospital and facilitates music therapy groups at Gateway Foundation for clients with chemical dependency and mental illness. Louise also leads drum circles and drumming workshops for professional organizations. She is a candidate for Fellowship in the Bonny Method of Guided Imagery and Music (GIM). Louise was a member of the faculty of The Old Town School of Folk Music. She has performed music to live audiences for more than 20 years. Her professional memberships include the American Music Therapy Association (AMTA) and The Association for Music and Imagery (AMI). Louise lives with her husband and seven year old daughter in Chicago, Illinois.

Dionisio-Pieczynski, Diana is the Manager of Publicity and Promotions at WGN-TV. She has worked at WGN for nearly a decade. She has a Bachelor of Science Degree in Advertising from the University of Illinois, Champaign-Urbana. She was named the Most Distinguished Graduate from her high school, Schaumburg High School. Diana is married and has one young son. Her birth date is April 20, 1966.

Emmerman, Emily K. is Vice President and Corporate Officer in charge of Strategic Services at Louis A. Weiss Memorial Hospital, University of Chicago Hospital. She received a Bachelor's Degree in Political Science in 1986 from the University of Michigan. She is married to Ross, a corporate attorney. Emily and Ross have a five year old son named Max and a one year old daughter named Natalie. Emily's birth date is August 13, 1964.

Frank, Ruby M. H. is the founder and president of Frank's Employment, Inc. She has served on the Delnor Community Hospital board for 36 years in addition to the St. Charles Chamber of Commerce, Baker Hotel Living Center, Aurora Foundation, Aurora University, WFXW-AM 1480 radio station, Kane DuPage Personnel, St.Charles Ambassadors, St. Charles Savings and Loan, St. Charles Historical Society, and the Dorchester Condo Association. Ruby also is a member of Women in Management, St. Charles Country Club, Bethlehem Lutheran Church, Illinois Association of Personnel Consultants, Women's Auxiliary of Delnor Community Hospital, Vocational Advisory of St. Charles School District #303, Business Department and Advisory Board of Waubonsee College, and GSB Women's Republican Club. Her awards include The Charlemagne Award, Executive of the Year 1982, Boy Scouts of America's Distinguished Citizen Award, Who's Who in Finance and Industry, Who's Who in American

Women, Who's Who in Midwest, and Who's Who in Executive and Professional Women. Ruby lives in St. Charles, Illinois and Naples, Florida. She has four grandchildren; Amanda Frank, Nicholas Frank, Dawn Dodge, and Carinna Dodge. Ruby is 77 years old.

Freeland, Kathleen S. is a horticulturist, lecturer, writer, and the manager of marketing for Midwest Groundcovers. She has participated in a number of professional organizations including the International Plant Propagator's Society, American Rose Society, American Rhododendron Society, Worcester County Horticultural Society, American Rock Garden Society, National Women in Horticulture, Illinois Certified Nurseryman, and the Perennial Plant Association. Kathleen is the recipient of the International Plant Propagator's Society Fellowship Award and the Illinois Certified Nurseryman of the Year, 1996. She has a Masters degree from Julliard and a Bachelor of Arts degree from the University of Wyoming. Kathleen has two grown sons and lives in St. Charles, Illinois. She is 60 years old.

Gerber Lewis, Harriet is the chairman of the board of Gerber Plumbing Fixtures, Corp., a plumbing fixtures manufacturer with close to 115 million dollars in sales. Active in volunteerism and philanthropy, Harriet has participated in many charitable organizations including the Dorothy Kahn group, the North Shore Auxiliary of the Jewish Children's Bureau, Mount Sinai Hospital Service Club, Brandeis University, Jewish Federation of Metropolitan Chicago, Jewish United Fund, American-Israel Political Action Committee, Hillel-CAYS Lewis Summer Intern Program, American/Israel Chamber of Commerce and Industry, U.S. Holocaust Memorial Museum, and Miseracordia. She has been honored with the Julius Rosenwald and Deborah Awards, and is the only woman to have been elected to the National Plumbing Hall of Fame. Harriet is a graduate from Northwestern University with a Bachelor of Arts Degree. She is a widow with three adult children, six grandchildren, and two great grandchildren. She lives in Winnetka, Illinois. Harriet was born in 1919.

Hahn L.N.C., Linaya is a health educator, public speaker, and author. She is the founder of the PMS Holistic Center and author of *PMS-Solving the Puzzle* that offers information on identifying and addressing the causes of premenstrual syndrome. She also is the founder of the PMS Holistic Center Charitable Fund, an organization that provides health scholarships for women, public education, professional education, capital development, and research. She has addressed the American College of Obstetricians and Gynecologists, been published in journals, and is regularly interviewed on radio and television as well as in newspapers and magazines. Linaya received her Bachelor of Arts degree from Washburn University and is a Licensed Nutrition Counselor. She is continuing her education through Bastyr University. Linaya is a life member and former branch president of the American Association of University Women (AAUW). She is the founder of Light for Health, which supplies full spectrum light boxes, tubes, and bulbs. Linaya has two adult sons, Christopher and Gregory Back, and lives in Buffalo Grove, Illinois. Her birth date is June 11, 1942.

Havey, Carol is the author of *Women and Self-Confidence: How to Take Charge of Your Life* and public speaker on women and self-esteem. She is a member of Toastmasters. Carol has degrees in nursing, fashion design, and art. Her hobbies include dancing, traveling, and gardening. She has seven children. Carol lives with her husband in La Grange, Illinois. She is 63 years old.

Hayden, Jane is the Director of Traffic at WGN-Television. She has been a WGN employee since 1980 and was awarded employee of the Year 1989. Jane is an executive board member of the Cotter Club division of the Boys 'n Girls Club. She coordinated a mentoring program with WGN-TV and Cotter Boys and Girls Club. Previously she was a mentor and board member of the Fourth Presbyterian Church mentoring program. She is an active political campaign volunteer. Jane was born on February 2, 1962.

Holstein, Ph.D., Sue (Susan) M. is a licensed clinical psychologist and hypnotherapist in private practice in Geneva, Illinois. Sue's practice includes therapy for clients of all age. She is also a public speaker on topics such as health and wellness, motivation, goal setting, women's issues, self-esteem, confidence, assertiveness, creativity, imagery, and visualization. Her academic credentials include a Ph.D. from the Illinois Institute of Technology, Masters Degree in rehabilitation psychology from the Illinois Institute of Technology, Masters Degree in Educational Psychology from Loyola University, and an undergraduate degree in Psychology from DePaul University. Sue is a member of the Geneva Chamber of Commerce, Geneva Women in Business, St. Charles Chamber of Commerce, American Psychological Association, Illinois Psychological Association, and the American Society of Clinical Hypnosis. She is married to Mark Holstein, an attorney. Sue and Mark also are magic stage illusionists and stage hands. They perform at corporate functions and offer motivational talks with a touch of magic. Sue's birth date is January 12, 1961.

Jillian, Ann is an actress, singer, and motivational speaker. She is a three time Emmy nominee and a Golden Globe award winner. Her acting career began at the age of six with appearances on Art Linkletter's TV shows. Her first major role was "Little Bo Peep" in Walt Disney's *Babes in Toyland*. Other feature film credits include *Mr. Mom* and *Gypsy*. Ann starred in at least 25 television movies, mini-series, and series including *The Ann Jillian Story, It's a Living, Jennifer Slept Here*, and *The Ann Jillian Series* and co-starred in *Ben Casey, Twilight Zone, Walt Disney's Wonderful World of Color*, and *Hazel*. She performed with Bob Hope on many television specials and USO tours. Ann made her Broadway debut in *Sugar Babies* with Mickey Rooney. Her musical credits include a CD, *Ann Jillian, In the Middle of Love* and numerous stage presentations. Her motivational lecture program, *The Winner in You*, combines humor and music with information about life, health, and the joys of being a mother. Ann performs for a number of charity organizations and is an active volunteer at her son's school and her church. She attended Valley College majoring in interior design. Ann also studied acting and music at the Los Angeles Civic Light Opera. She was born in Cambridge, Massachusetts and currently lives in Los Angeles. Her husband, Andy Murcia, is also her manager. Ann and Andy have a young son, Andrew Joseph H. Nauseda Murcia the IV.

Junceau, Barbara J. is a professional astrologer for personal and spiritual counseling. Under the name of Inner Light Astrology, she offers readings to clients world wide from diverse backgrounds and professions. She is a nationally recognized teacher and keynote speaker on astrology and metaphysics. Barbara is currently writing her third book titled *Astrology and the Evolution of Consciousness*. Her past employment includes positions in a campus ministry, the YWCA, The Commons: An Institute for the Independent Sector, an insurance agency, a hospital treatment center for substance abuse, and in municipal government. Barbara has a Masters Degree in Theology from Andover Newton Theological School and a Bachelor of Arts degree from Keuka College, New York. Her awards include Outstanding Young Women of America and several honor societies. Her memberships include the American Federation of Astrologers, International Society for Astrological Research, National Committee for Geocosmic Research, Association for Research and Enlightenment, and the Association for Astrological Networking. Barbara was born in New York state and has resided in Illinois since 1967.

Lampert, Eta-Lyn is the executive assistant to Master Magician Lance Burton. Previously, she was a professional dancer with Ringling Brothers Circus. Eta-Lyn is a native of Long Island, New York. She currently lives in Las Vegas, Nevada. She is 29 years old.

Martens, M.D., D.Ht., Ruth is a medical doctor in general practice. She specializes in classical homeopathy, a 200 year-old medical science founded in Germany and based on the patient's symptoms rather than the disease diagnosis. Ruth received her Medical Degree from the University of Health Services Chicago Medical School (now known as Finch University of Health Services/Chicago Medical School) and her Bachelor of Arts degree in psychology from Northwestern University. She is currently treasurer of the American Institute of Homeopathy, treasurer of the American Institute of Homeopathy Foundation, assistant editor of the American Institute of Homeopathy Journal, and faculty member of the National-Lincoln School of Post Graduate Education/National College of Chiropractic. She is in private practice in Wheaton, Illinois. Ruth is also an airplane pilot.

Martens Sorrentino, D.D.S., Jeannette B. is an independent dentist with Zachary Soiya, DDS and Associates. She received her Doctoral of Dental Surgery degree from Loyola University School of Dentistry, Masters of Science Degree from DePaul University, and Bachelor of Science degree from St. Mary's College, Notre Dame, Indiana. Her honors include the Searle Scholarship Award and Alpha Sigma Nu, Jesuit Honor Society, Loyola University award. She is a member of the American Dental Association, Illinois State Dental Association, and the Chicago Dental Society. Jeannette is active in many of her children's classroom and school activities. She is married to Matthew Sorrentino, a cardiologist. They have three young daughters, Katrina, 9 years old, Alyssa, 7 years old, and Georgina, 5 years old. They live in River Forest, Illinois. Jeannette is 42 years old.

McElroy, R.N., B.S.N., M.P.H., Debbie (Debra) is an independent registered nurse. She specializes in case management and received a masters degree in Public Health from Benedictine University in 1999. She received her Bachelor of Science Degree in Nursing from Marycrest College (now Marycrest International University) in 1977. Debbie is married to Terrence McElroy. They have three children. Debbie is 44 years old.

McNally, Ed.D., Theresa is a psychotherapist in private practice in Cambridge and Arlington, Massachusetts. She has worked in the field of mental health since she was 18 years old. Theresa works with children, adolescents, families and couples as well as individual clients. She incorporates psychoneuroimmunlogy and Spiritual traditions involving Eastern Buddhist meditation, yoga, and Christian Centered prayer and meditation into her practice. Theresa graduated from Boston University School of Education with a Doctorate in Counseling Psychology, Harvard University School of Education with a Masters Degree, and Drake University with a Bachelor Degree in Social Science. Theresa's husband is a child therapist and international consultant. Theresa and her husband have two wonderful children, Joanna, 13, and Will, 8 years old. Theresa is 48 years old.

Miller, Carole is a Realtor/broker. She currently is with Realty Executives in Geneva, Illinois. Carole is the President of the Women's Council of Realtors and Director of the Fox Valley Board of Realtors. She has received numerous service awards and Realtors designations in CRS, GRI, and LTG. Previously, Carole was the principal and administrator of special education at a state boys school and correctional facility. She has Masters of Science Degree and a Bachelor of Science Degree in Education and Administration from Illinois State University. Carole has two sons: Tom, born February 2, 1962 and David, born November 17, 1962. She also has two grandchildren, Alex and Callie Marie. Carole's birth date is December 15, 1943.

Oler, Sandy is a volunteer for Fox Valley Christian Church. She is a Bible study leader and active on many church committees. Sandy received her Bachelor's Degree from Purdue University. She is married to Kevin Oler. Sandy and Kevin have three children and live in St. Charles, Illinois.

Orman, Teresa is salon owner and hairstylist at New Images in Geneva, Illinois. She received her certification in 1979. Theresa specializes in hair coloring techniques. She is married and has three children. Teresa volunteers for numerous activities in which her children are involved.

Patch, Ph.D., Diana Craig is an archeologist who specializes in ancient Egyptian culture. She currently holds the position of Gallery Administrator in the Department of Egyptian Art at the Metropolitan Museum of Art in New York. She received her Doctorate Degree from the University of Pennsylvania's Department of Asian and Middle Eastern Studies with a focus in Egyptology, a Masters Degree in Anthropology from the Ohio State University, and a Bachelor of Arts Degree Magna Cum Laude from Washington University with majors in Anthropology and Geology. She has received numerous grants and scholarships and published articles and a book. Diana has taught courses in ancient Egyptian culture and archeology at Hunter College, City University of New York, Rutgers, The State University, University of Pittsburgh, and the Ohio

State University. She first undertook archeological field work in 1971 and has participated in several archaeological excavations in the United States and Iran. Since 1979, she has worked exclusively in Egypt, and is currently directing an excavation at the ancient Egyptian capital of Memphis. Diana is fluent in Arabic. Born February 3, 1954, Diana now lives in East Rockaway, New York with her husband and daughter.

Schellenberger, S.S.C.M., Sister Mary Stella entered the French order Servants of the Holy Heart of Mary in 1949. The order is based in Kanakakee, Illinois. She received a Masters Degree of Education from Seattle University, Seattle in 1974 and Bachelor of Arts degree from DePaul University, Chicago, in 1963. Sister Mary Stella retired in 1998 after 25 years as Religious Education Director of St. Peter Catholic Church. She also was a full time music and piano teacher, classroom teacher, and DRE. Sister Mary Stella is a fine artist, specializing in painting, and enjoys flower gardening. She was born in Indiana on December 8, 1931.

Schreter, Susan is the president of Seattle-based Caring Products International, a publicly traded marketer of cost-effective absorbent products. The company's patented Rejoice brand incontinence products are available in over 10,000 drug stores in North America and entering international markets. Susan is the creator of the WizzKidz toilet training product line, which has been licensed to Hasbro/Playskool as well as a product that has been selected by NASA for use within astronaut space suits. Prior to co-founding Caring Products, Susan served for seven years as president of Beta International, a firm providing acquisition consulting services to businesses primarily in the environmental clean-up industry. Susan is an active member of the Young Entrepreneur's Organization. She is an honors graduate of Smith College.

Scordo, Laurie is the founder of Laurel Gifts, a company which designs custom gift baskets. Laurie belongs to the National Association of Female Executives (NAFE), Council for Working Women, the Joliet Region Chamber of Commerce, and Rotary Club. She received the Certificate of Achievement 1997 and 1998 from Jubilee, Design Competition Outstanding Entry Award, and Certificate of Completion - Retail Sales and Service Performance Systems. She is married to Joe Scordo and has four children: Tony, 28 years old, Jennifer 26 years old, Joe, 20 years old, and Peter, 18 years old. She also has two "wonderful" grandsons, Michael and Andrew. Laurie's birth date is October 12, 1945.

Sharos, Ingrid is a supervisor for Adult Probations, DuPage County, IL. She also served as an adult and juvenile probations officer for the DuPage County Probation Department. She received a Masters degree in counseling and Bachelor of Science degree in sociology from Northern Illinois University. She has volunteered for many organizations including Community Coordinated Childcare and the American Red Cross. Ingrid is a school board member for Driscoll High School and an active member of the St. Isidore parish council. Ingrid and husband David have two children, Andrew, 13 years old and Nicole, 12 years old. They live in Carol Steam, Illinois. Ingrid is 45 years old.

Shepard, Linda is the director of Career Links, Women Employed's career-based group mentoring program for inner city teen girls. Prior to joining Women Employed in 1995, Linda was a legislative lobbyist and campaign consultant for over 20 years. She served eight years as San Francisco Bay Area Rapid Transit (BART) district's affirmative action officer, two four-year terms on the Alameda Contra Costa County Transit district Board of Directors, and as Vice President of Human Resources at the American Public Transit Association. Linda's honors and awards include being recognized by transit leaders for her organization and leadership, the National Council of Negro Women's Outstanding Business Leadership Award in 1987, The National Women's Political Caucus Leadership Award in 1989, U.S. Navy Woman of the Year Award, and the Metropolitan Transportation Commission's Special Letter of Recognition for the BART Summer Youth Programs.

Smith, Anita is a musical contractor and booking agent since 1962. She is president of Anita Smith Associates. She has contracted the music for plays, ballets, and singers such as *Phantom of the Opera, Les Miserables, Miss Saigon, Joseph*, Joffrey, Leningrad-Kirov ballet, *Beauty and the Beast, The Good-Bye Girl, Nutcracker*, and Luciano Pavarotti. Anita is 54 years-old and resides in Niles, Illinois with her much loved cats.

Storm, Rev. M. Sue is a minister with the World Congregational Fellowship. She is the founder of Angelight Productions, a spiritual advisor, and angelic facilitator. Sue is the author of *Angel First Aid: Rx for Miracles*. She has appeared on television programs such as *The Daily Show, Talk Soup, Fox News*, and *Hero T.V.* She is also the director of the Healthy Home Alliance, a foundation that educates the public on the health and safety risks of cellular towers. Sue is a member of the National Speakers Association and Professional Speakers of Illinois. She majored in psychology at the University of Michigan. Sue resides in Naperville, Illinois and has a daughter named Rochelle. Sue's birth date is April 15, 1942.

Sullivan, Pam (Pamela) J. is the Vice-President and General Manager of Technical and Training Services, Systems and Information Technology Group of TRW, Inc. She is responsible for long-term technology and information system support of the Defense Special Weapons Agency, On-Site Inspection Agency, Air Force Research Lab, and Air Force Air Logistics Center. Pamela offers technical guidance and evaluation of technical staff in information technology, training, mathematics, physics, and engineering disciplines throughout the country. She has executive cognizance for efforts ranging from military training and readiness, biological defense systems, military analyses, and Air Force logistics technologies. Pamela has a B.A. in Mathematics from Trinity College and is pursuing a graduate degree. She is married to Dr. Thomas A. Tumolillo. She has two children, Kelly and Dan. Pamela was born on January 28, 1945.

Tighe, Marlene is a communications consultant for non-profit organizations. Topics for presentations include the study of dialogue and feedback and fulfilling personal potential. She is completing her undergraduate degree at Ursuline College in Pepper Pike, Ohio with a major in Business Administration and a minor in Journalism. Her past experience includes management training and development, performance and process improvement concepts and developmental coaching. She was an Area Customer Service Manager at Ameritech specializing in the development of the Ameritech Self-Directed Work Team in Ohio. Marlene retired from Ohio Bell/Ameritech in 1993 after 36 years. She then consulted for Chrysler Corporation in their Customer One program. In 1995 Marlene returned to Ameritech as a business analyst in Chicago, Illinois. She serves as a volunteer on the Cleveland Heights Commission on Aging, board member on the Senior Computer Development Board, and a Trustee for the Cleveland Catholic Diocese Center for Pastoral Leadership. Marlene is 60 years proud.

Trent, Debra is a sculptor, performing artist, writer, and storyteller. She is a leader and educator for No Limits for Women Artists workshops. She also is an educator and special events coordinator for RCG. Her work has been featured in numerous exhibitions. Debra has received grant funds from KGP to support the writing about classism and art piece creation titled "White Girl's Cosmolog." Her awards include Supporting the Youth of Today award from Sherman Community Group, Annual Outstanding Community Activist award from Margaret Sloss Women's Center at Iowa State University, and Award for Community Enhancement, Women Empowered, a Force for the Future, YWCA, Iowa State University. She was an official representative of the Women's Caucus for Art at the United Nation's Fourth World Conference of Women in Beijing, China. Debra received her Bachelor of Arts degree in Art and Design, a minor in Women's Studies, and a minor in Anthropology from Iowa State University. She has completed some graduate classes at the University of Wisconsin and the Women's Theological Institute. Debra is a Wisconsin resident. She has four children: Shane-23 years old, Eon-22 years old, Justin 22 years-old, and Lance 15 years-old.

Umbach, Alice is a psychotherapist with 23 years of private practice experience. She specializes in treatment for adult children of alcoholics, individuals with sexual dysfunction, and victims of sexual, physical, and emotional abuse. She also provides marital and relationship counseling, individual and group therapy, and stress and anxiety therapy. Alice has taught classes at Oakton College, Harper College, and Greener Fields Unlimited. She conducts workshops and seminars on various women's issues. She belongs to the American Academy of Psychotherapy, American Academy of Certified Social Workers, National Association of Certified Social Workers, and Board Certified Diplomat. She received her MSW degree from Loyola University. Alice has three grown sons and three grandchildren. She lives in East Hampton, New York.

Webster, The Honorable Hollis L. is a circuit court judge, 18th Judicial Circuit, DuPage County, Illinois. She is currently assigned to Civil Law Jury Court. Her memberships include Strict Liability, Judicial Mentor Training, and Faculty National Institute of Trial Advocacy, DuPage County. Hollis previously served as an associate partner at Hinshaw and Culbertson and a clerk to the Honorable John A. Nordberg, Federal District Court. She has authored numerous legal articles in national, state, and local journals. Hollis is a graduate of National Judicial College (1993) Faculty for Domestic Violence Course. She received her Law Degree (J.D.) from Loyola University of Chicago (1982) and Bachelor of Science Degree in journalism from the University of Illinois in Champaign-Urbana (1997) with honors. She was a member of the Women's Intercollegiate Tennis Team, Production Manager of the Yearbook, and Mortar Board (scholastic and activities honor). Hollis is married to David, Chief Financial Officer at Brables U.S.A. They have three children, Michael, 15 years old, Benjamin, 12 years old, and Rachel, 9 years old. Hollis is a resident of Glen Ellyn, Illinois and was born on June 15, 1955.

Wheeler Hortum, Leslie is the senior Vice-President for federation development for the United States Chamber of Commerce. She is the first woman senior vice-president in the U.S. Chamber's 85 year history. Leslie attended the advanced management program at the University of Virginia's Darden School of Business and has an economics degree from Mary Washington College. She serves on the board of directors of World Child, Inc., an international adoption agency, and on the Board of Operation Enterprise, the youth development program of the American Management Association. Leslie is married to J.D. (John) Hortum, an Episcopal priest. They have two sons: Vanya, who is six years old and Dru, who is five years old.

Wilson Dickey, M.D., Nancy is President of the American Medical Association and a family physician in College Station, Texas. She is the program director for the Brazos Valley Family Practice program associated with Texas A&M University. She has chaired many medical committees and is a Fellow of the American Academy of Family Physicians. A graduate form the Stephen F. Austin State University, Nancy received her medical training at the University of Texas Medical School at Houston where she was the recipient of the Distinguished Alumni Award. She has served as a reviewer for the *Journal of the American Medical Association* and editorial advisor *of Patient Care, Medical World News* and *Medical Ethics Advisor*. She currently serves on the editorial board of *Archives of Family Medicine*. Nancy has taken an active role in numerous community activities such as coach for youth soccer and a sponsor for the United Methodist Youth Fellowship. She is a member of the Christ United Methodist Church. Nancy and her husband, Franklin (Champ), have three children, Danielle, Wilson, and Elizabeth.

Zecher, Rabbi Deborah is the spiritual leader of Hevreh of Southern Berkshire, a reform congregation, Union of American Hebrew Congregations. Her rabbinic ordination and Master of Hebrew Literature is from Hebrew Union College-Jewish Institute of Religion in New York. Deborah graduated from Brandeis University in 1973 with a degree in Near Eastern and Judaic Studies. She is currently the recording secretary of the Central Conference of American Rabbis. She is a member of the Women's Interfaith Institute of the Berkshires and associate member of the American Conference of Cantors. She is past national co-coordinator of the Women's Rabbinic Network. Deborah is married to Rabbi Dennis Ross. They have three children, Joshua, 13, Adam, 10, and Miriam, 10. Deborah's birth date is July 21, 1955.

APPENDIX

MENTORING PROGRAMS

Association of Small Business Development Centers
http//www.asbdc-us.org/delivery

Big Brothers/Big Sisters of America
It is recommended that you check your local directory for the agency nearest you. If you are unable to locate a local chapter, you may contact the organization at the following numbers:
230 N. 13th St.
Philadelphia, PA 19107
Tel: 215-567-7000

Career Links
Women Employed
22 West Monroe Street
  Suite 1400
Chicago, IL 60603
Tel: 312-782-3902

Guided Imagery and Music GIM
Association for Music and Imagery (AMI)
PO Box 4266
Blaine, WA 9823-4286
Tel: 360-756-8096
ami@nas.com

National SBDC Research Network
1222 N. Main St. #712
San Antoini, TX78212
Tel: 800-689-1912
E-mail: sbdcnet@utsu.edu

South West Women Working Together
4051 W. 63rd St.
Chicago, IL 60629
Tel: 312-582-0550

Cabrini Connections
Tutor/Mentor Connections
1111 N. Wells
  Suite 503
Chicago, IL 60610
Tel: 312-573-8851
Fax: 312-573-8816
www.tutormentorconnection.org

WITS Working In The Schools
Tel: 888-660-9487

INDEX

APPENDIX

WHO ARE YOUR HEROES?
WHO ASSISTED YOU WITH YOUR PERSONAL AND PROFESSIONAL GROWTH?

What have you learned from:

Family Members
Mother _____
_____
_____
_____
_____
_____
_____
_____

Father _____
_____
_____
_____
_____
_____
_____
_____

APPENDIX

Step-Mother _____

_____

_____

_____

_____

_____

Step-Father _____

_____

_____

_____

_____

_____

Sister/Sisters _____

_____

_____

_____

_____

_____

Brother/Brothers_____

_____

_____

_____

_____

_____

Step-Sister/Sisters _____

_____

_____

_____

_____

_____

WHO ARE YOUR HEROES?

Step-Brother/Brothers _____

_____
_____
_____
_____
_____

Grandmother _____

_____
_____
_____
_____
_____

Grandfather _____

_____
_____
_____
_____
_____

Step-Grandparents _____

_____
_____
_____
_____
_____

Aunt/Aunts _____

_____
_____
_____
_____

Uncle/Uncles _____

Cousins _____

Daughter/Daughters _____

Son/Sons _____

Step-Daughter/Daughters _____

WHO ARE YOUR HEROES?

Step-Son/Sons _____
_____
_____
_____
_____
_____

Niece/Nieces _____
_____
_____
_____

Nephew/Nephews _____
_____
_____

In-Laws _____
_____
_____
_____
_____

Peers
Spouse _____
_____
_____
_____
_____
_____
_____
_____

APPENDIX

Friends _____

_____

_____

_____

_____

_____

Co-Workers _____

_____

_____

_____

_____

_____

Neighbors _____

_____

_____

_____

_____

_____

_____

Teachers_____

_____

_____

_____

_____

_____

Coaches _____

_____

_____

_____

WHO ARE YOUR HEROES?

Fellow Club Members _____

_____

_____

_____

Bosses/Administrators _____

_____

_____

_____

_____

_____

Clergy/Spiritual Advisors _____

_____

_____

_____

_____

_____

Others
Shopkeepers _____

Librarians _____

Child-Care Providers _____

Assistants _____

Service Providers _____

ARE YOU A HERO?

Do you Mentor? _____

Who do you mentor? _____
_____
_____
_____
_____
_____

How do you mentor?_____
_____
_____
_____
_____
_____

What have you learned from your protégé? _____
_____
_____
_____
_____

Order Form

MENTORING HEROES
52 Fabulous Women's Paths to Success and the Mentors Who Empowered Them

Your Name: _____

Address:_____

City:_____State:_____Zip:_____

Telephone:_____

Please send:

_____copies of *MENTORING HEROES* @ $21.95 per copy

Subtotal: _____

6.5% Sales Tax-Illinois Residents Only: _____

Shipping and Handling   _____
($3 for the first book,
$2 for each additional book)

Total: _____

Send your check or money order to:
        3E Press
        P O Box 1004
        Batavia, IL 60510-1004

Order Form

MENTORING HEROES
52 Fabulous Women's Paths to Success and the Mentors Who Empowered Them

Your Name: _____

Address:_____

City:_____State:_____Zip:_____

Telephone:_____

Please send:

_____copies of *MENTORING HEROES* @ $21.95 per copy

Subtotal: _____

6.5% Sales Tax-Illinois Residents Only: _____

Shipping and Handling   _____
($3 for the first book,
$2 for each additional book)

Total: _____

Send your check or money order to:
        3E Press
        P O Box 1004
        Batavia, IL 60510-1004